EVERYONE'S GUIDE TO CHILDREN'S LITERATURE

MARK I. WEST

HIGHSMITH PRESS HANDBOOK SERIES

Highsmith
PRESS
Fort Atkinson, Wisconsin

Published by Highsmith Press LLC
W5527 Highway 106
P.O. Box 800
Fort Atkinson, Wisconsin 53538-0800
1-800-558-2110

© Mark I. West, 1997
Cover by Janet Robertson

The paper used in this publication meets the minimum requirements of American National Standard for Information Science —
Permanence of Paper for Printed Library Material. ANSI/NISO Z39.48-1992.

Library of Congress Cataloging-in-Publication Data

West, Mark I.
    Everyone's guide to children's literature / Mark I. West.
      p. cm. – (Highsmith Press handbook series)
    Includes bibliographical references and index.
    ISBN 0-917846-90-7
    1. Children's literature–History and criticism–Bibliography.
  2. Reference books–Children's literature–Bibliography. I. Title.
II. Series.
Z1037.A1W37 1997
[PN1009.A1]
011.62–dc21
                                               97-11717
                                                CIP

For my father, Walter H. West,

who is largely responsible for my love of literature

Contents

Acknowledgments

Over the course of writing this book, I drew on the advice, expertise and support of many people. The person who helped me the most is Pat Siegfried, the Director of Youth Services of the Public Library of Charlotte and Mecklenburg County. Pat introduced me to the world of listservs, assisted me with the bibliography, and made several suggestions that helped me broaden the scope of this book.

My aversion to computers is well known among my friends. It took a lot of coaching from several people to get me to the point where I could write the chapter on children's literature on the Internet. In addition to Pat, my other main computer coaches were Greg Wickliff and Donna White.

A number of people helped me with the bibliography, including Jan Susina, Lucy Rollin, Paula Connolly, and Anita Moss.

My wife, Nancy Northcott, read the first drafts of several of the chapters and made a number of good suggestions on how they could be improved. My preschool-aged son, Gavin, also made a good suggestion while I was writing this book, namely that I turn off the computer and tell him some more stories from the continuing saga of "Gavin and His Amazing Friends." I thank both Nancy and Gavin for their patience and support. And now it's time to return to Gavin and his Amazing Friends, who were last seen boarding Gavin's G-Wing fighter.

Elton'sPictorialABC.PublishedbyT.W.StongPublishers,
Boston, 1848.

Introduction

Chapter 1

I have been teaching college-level courses on children's literature for about fifteen years, and during that time I have come across over a dozen introductory books about children's literature. Although I have found many of these books to be useful, not one of them focuses on the practical information that my students often seek. Countless times students have asked me what reference sources they should use when doing research on a children's author or what journals publish articles about a particular aspect of children's literature. My graduate students often want to know what professional organizations they should consider joining or what libraries have special children's literature collections that relate to their research projects. Over the years, I have developed extensive files that I use when answering these sorts of questions, and one day it occurred to me that the information in my files could form the basis of a book. That's how I first came up with the idea of writing *Everyone's Guide to Children's Literature.*

Although I initially conceived of this book as a sort of supplementary text to be used in children's literature courses, my sense of the book's potential audience broadened after I talked about the book with a number of librarians, teachers, parents, book collectors and others interested in children's literature. Several librarians told me that they could use a handy guide to the key reference works on children's literature. Teachers said they wanted to know where they could find new ideas about incorporating children's literature in their curricular plans. Parents wanted to know how they could find out about new books that might appeal to their children. Book collectors wanted to know how they could get into contact with other collectors who shared their love of a particular author's books. I listened carefully to these various people and then set out to write a book that would address their concerns and interests.

Each chapter is intended to help readers find answers to the various questions they have about children's literature. In the chapter on reference works, I describe 26 important reference works that deal with children's literature. I also discuss their strengths and explain how to use them. The next chapter focuses on journals that publish articles about children's literature. In addition to describing these publications, I supply subscription information. The next chapter is devoted to organizations that relate to children's literature. I discuss the history and nature of each organization and provide membership information. Chapter 5 deals with the Internet and its connections to children's literature, which is followed by a chapter on special children's literature collections at major libraries. The penultimate chapter provides information about the major awards in children's literature and lists the winners of these awards. *Everyone's Guide to Children's Literature* closes with a bibliography of important books about children's literature. All of these chapters contain information that is subject to change. In the interest of keeping this information as current as possible, I have agreed to revise this book every few years for as long as there is a demand for it.

Changes in the status and study of children's literature

While conducting the research for this book, I became increasingly aware of the problems that stem from the deep divisions that run through the field of children's literature. I had long known that courses in children's literature are not always taught in English departments, which is where these courses are taught at my university. In some cases, children's literature courses are offered in schools of library science or in education departments that deal with the teaching of reading. It was not until I began working on this book, however, that I realized that these divisions were the product of a long and complex history. In order to understand current attitudes toward children's literature, it is helpful to review this history.

During the nineteenth century, most men and women of letters took children's literature fairly seriously. Some of the leading writers of the period also wrote children's books, including Mark Twain, Nathaniel Hawthorne, John Ruskin, and Robert Lewis Stevenson. *Atlantic Monthly,* one of the most widely read and highly regarded magazines of the day, had three chief editors who were also children's authors: Thomas Bailey Aldrich, Horace Scudder and William Dean Howells. These editors made sure that children's books were prominently reviewed in the pages of *Atlantic.* Most other major magazines also regularly reviewed children's books. Several children's authors, such as Louisa May Alcott, ranked among the period's highest paid authors.[1]

During the early years of the twentieth century, however, the overall status of children's literature gradually declined. Publishers continued to bring out new children's books, but these books attracted less and less attention from the general press. This trend continued unabated until a group of librarians began a concerted campaign to promote children's literature. Led by Anne Carroll Moore, these librarians advocated for the establishment of children's rooms in public libraries, published articles and books about children's literature, and began teaching courses on the subject to other librarians.[2]

This movement also led to the establishment of the Newbery Medal in 1922. Given by the Children's Librarians Section (now called the Association of Library Service to Children) of the American Library Association, the Newbery Medal has been given each year to a book that, in the opinion of the selection committee, is "the most distinguished contribution to American literature for children." The Newbery Medal quickly became the most prestigious award in the field. In 1938, this same organization began awarding the Caldecott Medal to distinguished picture books.[3]

Another development that grew out of these librarians' efforts to promote children's literature was the founding of *The Horn Book Magazine* in 1924. This was the first magazine devoted entirely to children's literature. In addition to publishing articles, it ran numerous reviews of children's books. Its founding editor, Bertha E. Mahony, intended it to function as an independent publication, and throughout its history it has never had any official ties to the American Library Association or any other professional library organization. Nevertheless, it soon emerged as an important organ for children's librarians. Since the magazine's inception, countless librarians have used these reviews when selecting books for their libraries.[4]

In 1942, the American Library Association began publishing another periodical intended for children's librarians. Entitled *Top of the News*, this quarterly included news about the various divisions of ALA that dealt with children, articles about children's authors, recommendations of books to include in libraries for children, and bibliographies of children's books relating to particular themes. *Top of the News* ceased publication in 1987 and was replaced by the *Journal of Youth Services in Libraries.*[5]

From the 1920s through the mid-1950s, children's librarians were the primary supporters of children's books. In the late 1950s, however, reading teachers began joining the efforts to enhance the status of children's literature. These teachers were responding in part to a growing controversy over the use of basal readers.

The novelist John Hersey helped spark this controversy when he published an article in *Life* in 1954 entitled "Why Do Students Bog Down on the First R?" In this article, Hersey called basal readers "pallid primers" and went on to state that most children would rather read a comic book than an "antiseptic little sugarbook showing how Tom and Betty have fun at home and school." He argued that children should be encouraged to read stories that deal in an imaginative way with "life's realities." Although he did not dwell on the point, he suggested that reading teachers should introduce children to a variety of stories, including the old, unedited versions of fairy tales.[6]

A number of teachers agreed with Hersey's main points and began making a concerted effort to use works of children's literature in reading programs. This movement took a big step forward in 1961 with the publication of Charlotte Huck and Doris Young's influential textbook *Children's Literature in the Elementary School.* This book was widely used in the training of new teachers and helped create a new generation of reading teachers who believed in the importance of including children's literature in the elementary school curriculum.

A New Zealand educator named Sylvia Ashton-Warner built an entire teaching philosophy around the idea of immersing students in literature and other forms of language. She articulated this philosophy in her 1963 book, *Teacher.* In the 1970s and '80s, a number of other educators, including Jeannette Vetch, Don Holdaway, Kenneth Goodman, and Yetta Goodman, amplified on Ashton-Warner's approach to teaching. Eventually, this approach came to be known as the literature-based or whole language teaching philosophy.

By the mid-1980s, literature-based teaching had achieved wide-spread acceptance among reading teachers. Most universities and colleges that trained teachers began requiring education students to take at least one or two courses on the philosophy and techniques of literature-based teaching. Moreover, the two major organizations in the field—the International Reading Association and the National Council of Teachers of English—promoted this approach in their publications and activities.[7]

About a decade after Huck and Young called for the inclusion of children's literature in the elementary school curriculum, Francelia Butler, an English Professor from the University of Connecticut, began arguing that children's literature should also be taught in college-level English courses. She felt that humanists should not only teach courses in children's literature, but they should also conduct scholarly studies of children's books. In 1972, she founded a journal called *Children's Literature*, and she expressed her views in an editorial published in the very first issue:

> *Children's literature is almost entirely in the hands of those in education or library science, who emphasize the uses of literature in the classroom, methodology, biographies of current writers, graded reading lists, book reports— good things but not the concern of those in the Humanities. What, then, should be the concern of humanists? Perhaps more than any other literature, they should be concerned with the quality of the literature available to our children and youth.* [8]

The year after *Children's Literature* debuted, Butler held a meeting with several other scholars who shared her interest in children's literature, including Anne Devereaux Jordan and Bennett Brockman. This group formed the Children's Literature Association and laid plans for a conference to be held in 1974. This conference brought together an energetic group of English professors and other scholars from the United States and Canada. In addition to agreeing to meet on an annual basis, the participants in the first Children's Literature Association Conference set an ambitious agenda designed to promote the serious study of children's literature. They officially linked the Association to Butler's journal, founded the *Children's Literature Association Newsletter* (which later evolved into the *Children's Literature Association Quarterly*), and began what proved to be a successful campaign to establish a children's literature division in the Modern Language Association.[9]

During the 1970s and early 1980s, literary critics and scholars who specialized in children's literature often found themselves in conflict with their colleagues who specialized in more "respectable" fields of literature. In colleges and universities all over North America, battles were waged over whether or not children's literature courses should be taught in English departments. Additional battles were fought over whether or not English professors who published scholarship on children's literature could count this scholarship when making their cases for tenure or promotion.

More often than not, the children's literature specialists won their battles. Children's literature courses are now taught in scores of English departments in the United States and Canada. *Children's Literature*, the journal founded by Butler, is now affiliated with Yale University Press, one of the nation's most prestigious university presses. *The Lion and the Unicorn*, another major academic journal devoted to literary studies of children's literature, began publishing in the late 1970s, and is now officially sponsored by Johns Hopkins University Press. Moreover, a number of highly regarded university presses have recently begun to publish scholarly books on children's literature. The most notable of these presses is the University of Georgia Press, which has brought out nearly an entire shelf of books about children's literature.

Since the early the 1990s, newcomers to the field of children's literature have been confronted with a problem that their predecessors could not have imagined twenty years ago. Instead of a dearth of material about children's literature, there is now such a large and diverse body of scholarship and reference materials related to children's literature that it is difficult to know where to start one's research. To make matters worse, there is surprisingly few connections among the major divisions in the field. Kathleen G. Short commented on this problem when she and her collaborators compiled a bibliography of recent scholarship on children's literature. "We were surprised," she wrote, "to find that researchers in different fields seemed to lack knowledge about one another's work. Researchers whose major focus was either library science, English education, literary criticism, reading education, or children's literature rarely cited work from other disciplines."[10]

One of my reasons for writing *Everyone's Guide to Children's Literature* is to inform newcomers to children's literature about some of the key resources, information, and scholarship related to this burgeoning field. I also hope, however, that this book will be of use to established children's literature specialists who are interested in bridging the disciplinary divisions within the field. Even though I am trained as a literary critic, I have great respect for the work of my colleagues in library science and education, and I have tried, in the pages of this book, to give equal treatment to each of these three major divisions. In a very real sense, the intended audience for *Everyone's Guide to Children's Literature* is everyone who takes children's literature seriously.

Notes

1. Anne H. Lundin and Carol W. Cubbberly, *Teaching Children's Literature: A Resource Guide, with a Directory of Courses* (Jefferson, North Carolina: McFarland, 1995), 8.

2. Cornelia Meigs et al., *A Critical History of Children's Literature* (New York: Macmillan, 1953), 420.

3. Meigs, 430.

4. Meigs, 422.

5. Marilyn H. Karrenbrock, "A History and Analysis of *Top of the News*, 1942–1987," *Journal of Youth Services in Libraries,* 1 (fall 1987): 29–33.

6. John Hersey, "Why Do Students Bog Down on the First R?" *Life*, 24 (May 1954): 136–150.

7. Charlotte S. Huck, "Literature-Based Reading Programs: A Retrospective," *New Advocate*, 9 (winter 1996): 23–33.

8. Francelia Butler, "The Editor's High Chair," *Children's Literature*, 1 (1972): 7–8.

   9. Jill P. May, *Children's Literature and Critical Theory* (New York: Oxford University Press, 1995), 24–26.

   10. Kathleen G. Short et al., *Research and Professional Resources in Children's Literature: Piecing a Patchwork Quilt* (Newark, DE: International Reading Association, 1995), 2.

Watts' Divine Songs. Published by J. Babcock and Son, New Haven, Conn., 1824.

Key Reference Works Related to Children's Literature

Chapter 2

Once upon a time it was difficult to find accurate information about children's literature, but that time has passed. Since the mid-1970s, many reference works related to children's literature have been published. Some, such as *Something about the Author,* are multi-volume works that take up an entire library shelf. Others, such as the recently published *International Companion Encyclopedia of Children's Literature,* take the form of one weighty volume. A listing of all these reference works would have over one hundred entries. There are, however, 26 key reference works that I have found to be especially helpful. What follows are descriptions of these works. The first section deals with works that focus on authors, which is followed by a section that covers works that take a general approach. the next section deals with works that are organized by the titles of children's books, and the last section describes works that focus on criticism.

Works that focus on authors

Something about the Author Gale Research began publishing this ongoing series in 1971. As its founding editor, Anne Commire, stated in the first volume, the series is intended to provide readers with an "almost personal introduction to authors." Every volume includes entries on one hundred or more children's authors or illustrators. Each entry provides key biographical information, the addresses of the author and/or the author's agent, an overview of the author's career, a listing of the awards and honors the author has received, a chronological bibliography of the books written or illustrated by the author, and information about other published sources that focus on the author. The entries are arranged alphabetically within each volume. There are cumulative indexes at the back of every other volume of the series—one for authors and the other for illustrators. To locate an entry about a particular author, readers should look up the author's name in the most recently published volume of the series that has indexes. The indexes indicate which volume or volumes have entries on the author.

Something about the Author. v. 1 (1971)– . Detroit: Gale.

Since Gale Research brings out about four new volumes of this series each year, *Something about the Author* tends to provide the most current information of all the reference works that focus on children's authors. Consequently, it is often the best place to turn for information about authors who have recently emerged on the scene. Also, the series often publishes updated entries on authors whose careers span many years. For readers who are seeking scholarly analyses of a particular author's works, however, *Something about the Author* is not the best reference work available. The entries in this series tend to be short and aimed a general audience.

Something about the Author. Autobiography Series Gale Research began publishing this series in 1986. The entries in this series are written by the authors or illustrators themselves and usually run about 10,000 words. The subjects are given free rein when writing these entries. Some of the entries are fairly formal accounts of the subject's career, while others are very personal essays that delve into such subjects as the author's childhood or family life. These entries usually include photographs and other visual material. At the end of each entry is a bibliography of the author's works. There is a cumulative index at the back of each volume.

Something about the Author. Autobiography Series. v. 1 (1986)– . Detroit: Gale.

In most cases, the authors and illustrators included in this series have not written full-scale autobiographies. Thus, for readers who are interested in an author's thoughts about his or her life and career, this reference work is well worth consulting. Readers, however, should be aware that there are many children's authors and illustrators who are not included in this series.

Authors and Artists for Young Adults Gale Research began this series in 1989. It follows that same format as *Something about the Author,* but it focuses more on authors and illustrators whose works have a teenage audience. Many of the same authors that are included in *Authors and Artists for Young Adults* are also included in *Something about the Author.*

Authors and Artists for Young Adults. v. 1 (1989)– . Detroit: Gale.

As one would expect, *Authors and Artists for Young Adults* has entries on important young adult authors, such as Judy Blume, Robert Cormier, and Walter Dean Meyers. It also, however, includes entries on authors whose works are intended primarily for adults but are often read by teenagers, including William Faulkner, Hermann Hesse, Stephen King, Sam Shepard, Agatha Christie, and David Eddings.

Dictionary of Literary Biography. Of the various reference works published by Gale Research, this series is perhaps the most scholarly in tone. All the volumes in this series provide in-depth biographical essays which trace an author's writing career, discuss the evolution of the author's literary reputation, and appraise the author's major works. These essays are written by noted scholars. The volumes in this series are organized thematically. There are now eight volumes that focus on children's authors, four of which deal with American authors and four that deal with British authors. Another volume dealing with British children's authors is planned.

Dictionary of Literary Biography. Detroit: Gale, 1978– . (In progress)

Volume 22, titled *American Writers for Children, 1900-1960,* came out in 1983 under the editorship of John Cech. Among its 43 entries are essays on

L. Frank Baum, Margaret Wise Brown, Walt Disney, Esther Forbes, Lois Lenski, Marjorie Kinnan Rawlings, E. B. White, and Laura Ingalls Wilder.

Volume 42, titled *American Writers for Children Before 1900*, came out in 1985 under the editorship of Glenn E. Estes. Among its 52 entries are essays on Louisa May Alcott, Frances Hodgson Burnett, Mary Mapes Dodge, Joel Chandler Harris, Howard Pyle, Harriet Beecher Stowe, and Kate Douglas Wiggin.

Volume 52, titled *American Writers for Children Since 1960: Fiction*, came out in 1986 under the editorship of Glenn E. Estes. Among its 44 entries are essays on Lloyd Alexander, Judy Blume, Beverly Cleary, Robert Cormier, Louise Fitzhugh, Virginia Hamilton, Madeleine L'Engle, Lois Lowry, Katherine Paterson, Mildred Taylor, and Jane Yolen.

Volume 61, titled *American Writers for Children Since 1960: Poets, Illustrators, and Nonfiction Authors*, came out in 1987 under the editorship of Glenn E. Estes. Among its 32 entries are essays on Marcia Brown, Tomie dePaola, Theodor Seuss Geisel, Leo Lionni, Arnold Lobel, Milton Meltzer, Jack Prelutsky, Richard Scarry, Maurice Sendak, Peter Spier, William Steig, and Chris Van Allsburg.

Vol 141, titled *British Children's Writers, 1880–1914*, came out in 1994 under the editorship of Laura M. Zaidman. Among its 24 entries are essays on J. M. Barrie, Kenneth Grahame, Kate Greenaway, Rudyard Kipling, Andrew Lang, E. Nesbit, Beatrix Potter, Arthur Rackham, and Robert Louis Stevenson.

Volume 160, titled *British Children's Writers, 1914–1960*, came out in 1996 under the editorship of Donald R. Hettinga and Gary D. Schmidt. Among its 37 entries are essays on Enid Blyton, C. S. Lewis, Hugh Lofting, A. A. Milne, Mary Norton, J. R. R. Tolkien, P. L. Travers, and T. H. White.

Volume 161, titled *British Children's Writers Since 1960: First Series*, came out in 1996 under the editorship of Caroline C. Hunt. Among its 30 entries are essays on Joan Aiken, Susan Cooper, Helen Cresswell, Leon Garfield, Alan Garner, Dinan Wyne Jones, Philippa Pearce, and Margery Sharp.

Volume 163, titled *British Children's Writers, 1800–1880*, came out in 1996 under the editorship of Meena Khorena. Among its 40 entries are essays on William Blake, Randolph Caldecott, Lewis Carroll, Walter Crane, Charles Kingsley, Edward Lear, George MacDonald, Christina Georgina Rossetti, and Charlotte Mary Yonge.

Children's Literature Review When Gale Research inaugurated this series in 1976, its goal was to provide readers with a guide to the published criticism and commentary related to children's authors. Since its debut, *Children's Literature Review* has evolved into one of the most consulted reference works in the field. Each volume contains entries on eight to ten authors. A typical entry begins with a short overview of the author's life and career followed by a section called "Author's Commentary," which includes excerpts from interviews and articles in which the author discusses his or her own work. The next section provides excerpts from articles that take a general approach to the author's work. The final section of the entry deals with criticism and commentary pertaining to particular books by the author. For the most part, the material excerpted in

Children's Literature Review. [v.1] 1976– . Detroit: Gale,

this section comes from published book reviews. The sources of all the quotations in each entry are carefully identified. At the end of each volume, there are three cumulative indexes—one focuses on authors, another on book titles, and the third on the authors' nationalities. As is the case with most of reference works published by Gale, readers should always turn to the indexes included in the most recently published volume in the series.

When readers are using *Children's Literature Review,* they should keep in mind that most of the information included in the entries is excerpted from published sources. On occasion, not all of the information included in the original sources is reprinted in the excerpts. Thus, readers can often find additional information and insights by locating and reading the original sources from which these excerpts came.

Junior Book of Authors   Before Gale Research began publishing works on children's literature, the *Junior Book of Authors* was the best source for information about children's authors. When H. W. Wilson published the first volume of this series in 1934, it was the first major reference work to focus on children's authors. Compared to the entries in the *Something about the Author* series the entries in the *Junior Book of Authors* are not as fully developed. They tend to be only a few paragraphs long, and they do not include complete bibliographies of the authors' works. Nevertheless, this series is sometimes the only reference work to include information about lesser known children's authors from the first half of the twentieth century.

Volume one of the series, titled *The Junior Book of Authors,* came out in 1934 under the editorship of Stanley J. Kunitz and Howard Haycraft. It includes 268 entries, each of which is accompanied by photograph of the author. Many of the entries are written by the children's authors themselves. Kunitz and Haycraft edited a second edition of this volume, which appeared in 1951. The second edition includes 289 entries, 129 of which are new.

Volume two, titled *More Junior Authors,* came out in 1963 under the editorship of Muriel Fuller. It includes 268 entries, most of which focus on authors who achieved prominence during the 1950s and early '60s.

Volume three, titled *The Third Book of Junior Authors,* came out in 1972 under the editorship of Doris De Montreville and Donna Hill. It includes entries on 255 authors, most of whom achieved prominence during the 1960s and early '70s. Unlike the entries from the earlier volumes, each entry in this volume includes a bibliography of selected works by each author and a list of references that provide additional information about the author. This volume also includes a cumulative index to all the volumes in the series.

Volume four, titled *The Fourth Book of Junior Authors and Illustrators,* came out in 1978 under the editorship of Doris De Montreville and Elizabeth D. Crawford. It includes 239 entries, one third of which deal with illustrators. The entries on authors deal primarily with those who gained prominence during the mid-1970s, but there are entries on illustrators from a variety of periods. This volume includes a cumulative index.

Volume 5, titled *The Fifth Book of Junior Authors and Illustrators,* came out in 1983 under the editorship of Sally Holmes Holtze. It includes 239 entries on authors and illustrators, most of whom achieved prominence during the

Junior Book of Authors   2nd ed. Stanley J. Kunitz and Howard Haycraft, eds. New York: H.W. Wilson, 1951.

Continued by

More Junior Authors, 1963. Muriel Fuller, ed.

The Third Book of Junior Authors, 1972. Doris De Montreville and Donna Hill, eds.

The Fourth Book of Junior Authors and Illustrators, 1978. Doris De Montreville and Elizabeth D. Crawford.

The Fifth Book of Junior Authors and Illustrators, 1983. Sally Holmes Holtze, ed.

The Sixth Book of Junior Authors and Illustrators, 1989. Sally Holmes Holtze, ed.

late 1970s and early 1980s. This volume includes a cumulative index.

Volume 6, titled *The Sixth Book of Junior Authors and Illustrators*, came out in 1989 under the editorship of Sally Holmes Holtze. It includes 236 entries on authors and illustrators, most of whom achieved prominence during the 1980s. This volume includes a cumulative index.

Twentieth-Century Children's Writers   The third and most recent edition of this handy reference work was published by St. James Press in 1989. Edited by Tracy Chevalier, it includes 800 entries. These entries focus on twentieth-century, English-language authors who write fiction, poetry, or drama for children. Each entry includes key biographical information, a complete bibliography of the author's works, and a short discussion of the author's most important contributions to children's literature. The book also features an appendix that has entries on major nineteenth-century children's authors.

Nearly all of the authors included in *Twentieth-Century Children's Writers* are covered in more detail in *Something about the Author.* There are occasions, however, when readers would rather consult a one-volume book than deal with the complications involved in using a multi-volume work. For readers who are trying to track down the publication date of a particular book by a children's author, identify the nationality of an author, or find some other bit of specific information about an author, *Twentieth-Century Children's Writers* is a good source to consult.

Twentieth-Century Children's Writers. 3rd ed. Tracy Chevalier, ed. New York: St. James Press, 1989.

Children's Books and Their Creators   Published by Houghton Mifflin Company in 1995, *Children's Books and Their Creators* is a one-volume work that provides biographical and critical overviews of children's authors and illustrators. Anita Silvey, the book's editor, made a special effort to include entries on authors and illustrators who have come into print since World War II.

Although *Children's Books and Their Creators* is very similar to *Twentieth-Century Children's Writers*, there are some differences that are worth noting. The entries in *Children's Books and Their Creators* are generally longer and more analytical than the entries found in *Twentieth-Century Children's Writers.* The entries in Silvey's book, however, do not include the comprehensive bibliographies and lists of references that accompany all the entries in *Twentieth-Century Children's Writers.* Unlike *Twentieth Children's Writers*, Silvey's book also includes entries on subjects other than particular authors and illustrators. There are entries, for example, on Australian children's literature, awards and prizes, Canadian children's literature, comic books and graphic novels, controversial books for children, fantasy literature, Latino children's books, magazines for children, and poetry for children. Another special feature found in Silvey's book is a series of entries titled "Voices of the Creators" in which children's authors or illustrators discuss their lives and works.

Children's Books and Their Creators. Anita Silvey, ed. Boston: Houghton Mifflin, 1995.

Writers for Children: Critical Studies of Major Authors Since the Seventeenth Century   Edited by Jane M. Bingham, *Writers for Children* was published by Charles Scribner's Sons in 1988. It contains 84 lengthy essays on children's authors "who have withstood the test of time." All of the authors included in this volume are deceased and their major works have remained in print at

Writers for Children: Critical Studies of Major Authors Since the Seventeenth Century. Jane M. Bingham, ed. New York: Scribner's, 1988.

least two generations after their original publication date.

The entries in *Writers for Children* are very similar to the entries in the *Dictionary of Literary Biography* volumes pertaining to children's authors. Both of these reference works feature scholarly essays written by noted authorities in children's literature, and both reference works cover many of the same authors. However, since all of the existing *DLB* volumes focus on either American or British children's authors, there are a number of very important children's authors from other countries who cannot be found in the *DLB* volumes. To its credit, *Writers for Children* includes entries on several such authors, including Hans Christian Andersen, Jean de Brunhoff, Carlo Collodi, Jacob and Wilhelm Grimm, Lucy Maud Montgomery, Charles Perrault, Felix Salten, and Johanna Spyri.

Black Authors and Illustrators of Children's Books   When Garland Publishing brought out Barbara Rollock's *Black Authors and Illustrators of Children's Books* in 1988, it was the first reference work to have such a focus. Garland brought out an expanded second edition of this book in 1992. The second edition has entries on 150 authors and illustrators, including Ashley Bryan, Alice Childress, Lucille Clifton, Donald Crews, Rosa Guy, Virginia Hamilton, Dorlores Johnson, Julius Lester, Walter Dean Meyers, Jerry Pinkney, John Steptoe, Eleanora Tate, and Mildred Taylor.

Black Authors and Illustrators of Children's Books works especially well when it is used in conjunction with *Something about the Author*. Rollock's book does a good job of identifying African American authors and illustrators of children's books, including those who are lesser known or who are not easily identified as being Black. However, because the entries in this book are usually only two or three paragraphs long, they do not provide a lot of information. In many cases, readers can find additional information about these authors and illustrators in *Something about the Author*.

Black Authors and Illustrators of Children's Books: A Biographical Dictionary. 2nd ed. Barbara Rollock. New York: Garland, 1992.

Works that take a general approach

Dictionary of American Children's Fiction   Written by Alethea K. Helbig and Agnes Regan Perkins, *Dictionary of American Children's Fiction* is a three-volume work published by Greenwood Press. The first two volumes came out in 1985, and the third appeared in 1993. Helbig and Perkins provide entries on book titles, authors, major characters, and settings. Volume one focuses on children's literature that dates from 1859 to 1959. It features 1,266 entries based on 420 books. Volume two focuses on books that date from 1960 to 1984. It contains 1,550 entries based 489 books. The third volume deals with books that date from 1985 to 1989. It has 400 entries based on 134 books.

Dictionary of American Children's Fiction is intended to provide readers with key information. For readers who want to know what book a character comes from, when a book was published, who wrote a particular title, or where a story is set, *Dictionary of American Children's Fiction* is good place to turn for dependable answers.

Dictionary of American Children's Fiction 1859–1959: Books of Recognized Merit. Alethea K. Helbig and Agnes Regan Perkins. Westport, CT: Greenwood, 1985.

Continued by:

Dictionary of American Children's Fiction 1960–1984: Books of Recognized Merit. 1986.

Dictionary of American Children's Fiction 1985–1989: Books of Recognized Merit. 1993.

Dictionary of British Children's Fiction Written by Alethea K. Helbig and Agnes Regan Perkins, *Dictionary of British Children's Fiction* was published by Greenwood Press in 1989. Helbig and Perkins provide entries on book titles, authors, major characters, and settings. This work contains 1,626 entries based on 387 books published from 1678 to 1985.

Although not quite as comprehensive as the *Dictionary of American Children's Fiction*, Helbig and Perkin's *Dictionary of British Children's Fiction* is still a source of specific information about British children's books and their authors.

Dictionary of British Children's Fiction: Books of Recognized Merit. Alethea K. Helbig and Agnes Regan Perkins. Westport, CT: Greenwood, 1989.

Dictionary of Children's Fiction from Australia, Canada, India, New Zealand, and Selected African Countries Written by Alethea K. Helbig and Agnes Regan Perkins, this reference work was published by Greenwood Press in 1992. Helbig and Perkins provide entries on book titles, authors, major characters, and settings. It features 726 entries based on 263 books. In selecting which books to include in this work, Helbig and Perkins placed their emphasis on books that are written in English.

This book is one of the best reference works available that deals with children's literature from an international perspective.

Dictionary of Children's Fiction from Australia, Canada, India, New Zealand, and Selected African Countries: Books of Recognized Merit. Alethea K. Helbig and Agnes Regan Perkins. Westport, CT: Greenwood, 1992.

International Companion Encyclopedia of Children's Literature Edited by Peter Hunt, the *International Companion Encyclopedia of Children's Literature* was published by Routledge in 1996. This book is one of the only reference works in the field that does not focus on authors or individual titles. Instead, the book contains 86 scholarly essays which are organized around the following four subheadings: "Theory and Critical Approaches," "Types and Genres," "The Context of Children's Literature," and "The World of Children's Literature."

Among the ten entries in the section titled "Theory and Critical Approaches" are essays on reader-response criticism, psychoanalytic criticism, feminist criticism, and illustration and picture books.

Among the 26 entries in the section titled "Types and Genres" are essays on fairy and folk tales, playground rhymes, poetry, drama, animal stories, high fantasy, science fiction, family stories, school stories, historical fiction, and children's magazines.

Among the eighteen entries in the section titled "The Context of Children's Literature" are essays on children's book publishing in Britain, children's book publishing in the United States, censorship, prizes and prizewinners, librarianship, and bibliotherapy.

Among the 31 entries in the section titled "The World of Children's Literature" are essays on children's literature from France, Spain, Germany, Italy, Russia, Eastern Europe, Israeli, the Arab world, Africa, China, Japan, Australia, New Zealand, and Canada.

International Companion Encyclopedia of Children's Literature. Peter Hunt, ed. New York: Routledge, 1996.

Oxford Companion to Children's Literature Written by Humphrey Carpenter and Mari Prichard, this single-volume work was published by Oxford University Press in 1984. Carpenter and Prichard deal with children's literature from Britain, United States, Canada, Australia, and New Zealand. Their book includes nearly 2,000 entries, about 900 of which focus on authors or illustrators. There are also entries are on important books, major children's magazines, famous characters from children's literature, and other related topics.

Oxford Companion to Children's Literature. Humphrey Carpenter and Mari Prichard. New York: Oxford University Press, 1984.

As its title suggests, *Oxford Companion to Children's Literature* is a useful book to keep on hand while one is reading about children's literature. On such occasions, one often comes across references to unfamiliar books or authors. In most cases, basic information about these books and authors can be found in the *Oxford Companion to Children's Literature.* Carpenter and Prichard are British, which perhaps explains why their book is especially strong when it comes to British children's literature.

Works that focus on titles

Touchstones: Reflections on the Best in Children's Literature   Edited by Perry Nodelman, this three-volume work was published by the Children's Literature Association. Unlike the many reference works that focus on children's authors, *Touchstones* contains scholarly essays on individual books for children.

Touchstones: Reflections on the Best in Children's Literature. Perry Nodelman, ed. West Layfayette, IN: Children's Literature Association, 1985.

Volume one, which was published in 1985, focuses on classic novels for children. Among its 28 entries are essays on Louisa May Alcott's *Little Women*, Lewis Carroll's *Alice's Adventures in Wonderland*, Frances Hodgson Burnett's *The Secret Garden*, Louise Fitzhugh's *Harriet the Spy*, Esther Forbes's *Johnny Tremain*, Robert O'Brien's *Mrs. Frisby and the Rats of NIMH*, Robert Louis Stevenson's *Treasure Island*, J. R. R. Tolkien's *The Hobbit*, Mark Twain's *The Adventures of Tom Sawyer*, and E. B. White's *Charlotte's Web*.

Volume two, which was published in 1987, deals with collections of fairy tales, myths, legends and poetry. Among its 20 entries are essays on Richard Chase's *Jack Tales*, Joel Chandler Harris's *Tales of Uncle Remus*, Andrew Lang's *The Blue Fairy Book*, Edward Lear's *Book of Nonsense*, and Howard Pyle's *The Merry Adventures of Robin Hood*.

Volume three, which was published in 1989, deals with picture books. Among its 19 entries are essays on Wanda Ga'g's *Millions of Cats*, Ezra Jack Keats's *The Snowy Day*, Robert McCloskey's *Make Way for Ducklings*, Beatrix Potter's *The Tale of Peter Rabbit*, Maurice Sendak's *Where the Wild Things Are*, and Dr. Seuss's *The Five Hundred Hats of Bartholomew Cubbins*.

Beacham's Guide to Literature for Young Adults   Edited by Kirk H. Beetz and Suzanne Niemeyer, this five-volume series was published the Walter Beacham Company between 1989 and 1991. The series contains entries on about 400 books for older children and adolescents. Most of the entries are on novels, but it also includes entries on short story collections, biographies, autobiographies, and a few works of nonfiction.

Beacham's Guide to Literature for Young Adults. Kirk H. Beetz and Suzanne Niemeyer, eds. Washington, D.C.: Beacham Pub., 1989-1991.

Although this series is intended for a general audience, it is especially well suited for students who are doing research projects on particular books. All of the entries follow a format that young readers can easily understand. Each entry is divided into ten subsections. The first section deals with the author's life and career, which is followed by an overview of the book's contents. The third section discusses the book's setting, and the fourth deals with the themes and characters found in the book. The next sections address the book's literary qualities and its potential for sparking controversy. The subheadings for the final four sections are "Topics for Discussion," "Ideas for Reports and Papers," "Related Titles/Adaptations," and "For Further Reference."

This Land Is Our Land: A Guide to Multicultural Literature for Children and Young Adults   Written by Alethea K. Helbig and Agnes Regan Perkins, this one-volume work was published by Greenwood Press in 1994. Helbig and Perkins provide annotations for 559 books published from 1985 through 1993. Although most of these books are novels, there are also annotations on collections of stories from the oral tradition and works of poetry. *This Land Is Our Land* is organized around four major ethnic groups within the United States: African Americans, Asian Americans, Hispanic Americans, and Native American Indians.

This Land Is Our Land: A Guide to Multicultural Literature for Children and Young Adults. Alethea K. Helbig and Agnes Regan Perkins. Westport, CT: Greenwood, 1994.

Our Family, Our Friends, Our World: An Annotated Guide to Significant Multicultural Books for Children and Teenagers   Written by Lyn Miller-Lachmann, this guide was published by R. R. Bowker in 1992. It begins with annotations about children's books dealing with four major ethnic groups within the United States. The second half deals with children's books dealing with different regions of the world. Each annotation includes a plot summary and an evaluation of the book. The book closes with an extensive index.

Our Family, Our Friends, Our World: An Annotated Guide to Significant Multicultural Books for Children and Teenagers. Lyn Miller-Lachmann. New Providence, NJ: R.R. Bowker, 1992.

World Historical Fiction Guide for Young Adults   Edited by Lee Gordon and Cheryl Tanaka, this book was published by Highsmith Press in 1995. Gordon and Tanaka provide entries on 800 historical novels written for young adults. The book includes entries on classic novels as well as works written more recently. Each entry provides a full bibliographic citation, a summary of the plot, a note about the book's setting, and information about the book's reading level.

World Historical Fiction Guide for Young Adults. Lee Diane Gordon and Cheryl Tanaka. Fort Atkinson, WI: Highsmith Press, 1995.

A to Zoo: Subject Access to Children's Picture Books   The 4th edition of Carolyn and John Lima's *A to Zoo* was published by R. R. Bowker in 1993. *A to Zoo* is a frequently used by children's librarians because it helps them answer many of the questions they are asked. Often a child or a parent will approach a children's librarian and ask a question like the one I recently put to a librarian I know. "My son is interested in knights," I said. "Do you know of any picture books that feature knights?" She took out *A to Zoo*, looked under the heading of knights, and read me the titles of six books. In addition to knights, *A to Zoo* provides 800 other subject headings. Over 14,000 picture books for preschool children through second graders are listed in the book.

A to Zoo: Subject Access to Children's Picture Books. 4th ed. Carolyn W. Lima, John A. Lima. New Providence, NJ: R.R. Bowker, 1993.

Works that focus on criticism

Children's Literature: A Guide to the Criticism   Written by Linnea Hendrickson, *Children's Literature: A Guide to the Criticism* was published by G. K. Hall in 1987. Hendrickson provides publication information and brief annotations for articles, books, and dissertations relating to children's literature criticism. The book is divided into two major sections. Part A is titled "Authors and Their Works," and Part B is titled "Subjects, Themes, and Genres." Hendrickson also provides an "Index of Critics," and an "Index of Authors, Titles, and Subjects." Most of the sources cited in this book date between 1970 and 1986, although some older sources are also included.

Children's Literature: A Guide to Criticism. Linnea Hendrickson. Boston: G.K.Hall, 1987.

Research and Professional Resources in Children's Literature: Piecing a Patchwork Quilt   Edited by Kathy G. Short, *Research and Professional Resources in Children's Literature* was published by the International Reading Association in 1995. This is a good reference work to use in conjunction with Hendrickson's *Children's Literature: A Guide to the Criticism*. Like Hendrickson's guide, Short's book provides publication information and brief annotations for articles and books about children's literature, but Short's book focuses on the sources that were published between January 1985 and December 1993. Short also provides an author index and a subject index.

Research and Professional Resources in Children's Literature: Piecing a Patchwork Quilt. Kathy G. Short, ed. Newark, DE: International Reading Association, 1995.

Children's Literature Abstracts   Founded in 1973, *Children's Literature Abstracts* is published by the International Federation of Library Associations. Six issues of this publication come out each year. Four of these issues contain abstracts of articles that deal with children's literature, and the other two issues contain abstracts of recently published books and pamphlets. In most issues of *Children's Literature Abstracts* there are eighteen subheadings under which the abstracts are listed, including "Authors and Illustrators," "Awards, Prizes, and Organizations," "Curriculum, Instruction, and Bibliotherapy," "Fantasy and Science Fiction," "Historical and Sociological Studies," "National and Minority Literatures," "Nonfiction," "Poetry," and "Young Adult Literature."

Children's Literature Abstracts. no. 1 (May 1973)– . [Birmingham, England]: Sub-Section on Library Work with Children, International Federation of Library Associations. Quarterly.

The sources that are abstracted in this reference work come from a variety of countries. Consequently, American users of this reference work may have to use inter-library loan services to obtain copies of some of the articles that are summarized in *Children's Literature Abstracts.*

Children's Book Review Index   Gale Research has brought out a new volume of this reference work each year since 1975. *Children's Book Review Index* provides access to reviews of children's books published in about 175 periodicals. The entries are arranged by the names of the authors. An illustrator index and a title index can be found at the end of each volume.

Children's Book Review Index. v. 1 no. 1 (Jan./Apr. 1975)– . Detroit: Gale. Annual.

In order to use *Children's Book Review Index*, readers need to know the original publication date of the book that they are looking up. In addition to checking the annual volume that corresponds with the book's publication date, researchers should also check the next couple of volumes. The reason for this is that book reviews often come out a year or two after the book was first published.

The Horn Book Guide to Children's and Young Adult Books   Founded in 1989, *The Horn Book Guide* is published twice a year by the Horn Book Company. This reference work provides short critical annotations of all hardcover trade children's books published in the United States. The editors of *The Horn Book Guide* strive to cover each of these books no later than six months after its original publication. Every book that is covered is rated on a scale of one to six, with one being outstanding and six being unacceptable.

The Horn Book Guide to Children's and Young Adult Books. v. 1. no. 1 (July-Dec 1989)– . Boston: Horn Book, Inc. 2/yr.

The Horn Book Guide is an especially useful tool for librarians who are responsible for selecting the books to be included in the children's sections of libraries.

T H E

Juvenile Magazine;
O R, A N

INSTRUCTIVE and ENTERTAINING

MISCELLANY
F O R

YOUTH of BOTH SEXES.

For *January* 1788

Embellished with Two Prints; L'Enfant Docile; and the
Silly Boy.

C O N T E N T S.

The Editor's Address to her | The Young Miser.......... 27
Young Readers........ page iii | The Little Boy who behaved
An Easy Introduction to Geo- | Like a Man .... page 33
graphy.................. 5 | Instructive Puzzles—An
The School-Boy.......... 10 | Enigmatical Description of a
L'Enfant Docile .... 14 | Good Girl................ 36
Fire Side Dialogues—The Silly | Notes to the Instructive
Boy................... 15 | Puzzles................ 35
Familiar Letters on Various | The Little Foreigner; a
Subjects—From Miss *Travelove* | Drama in One Act 37
to Mrs. *Wingrove*—From Miss | Poetry.................. 55
Travelove to *Phillis Flowerdale* 22 | Monthly Occurrences 57

Printed and Published by and for
J. Marshall and Co.,
Aldermary Church-Yard, Bow-Lane, Cheapside, London.
To whom COMMUNICATIONS (*Post paid*) are requested to be
addressed; and by whom any Hints for the Improvement of the Publi-
cation, will be thankfully received.

Journals and Periodicals Related to Children's Literature

Chapter 3

While conducting the research for this chapter, I asked a number of children's literature specialists to name all of the children's literature journals with which they were familiar. In most cases, they listed seven or eight journals, but the ones that they mentioned varied considerably. The librarians with whom I spoke often listed *Horn Book, Journal of Youth Services in Libraries,* and *Book Links.* The reading specialists cited such journals as *Teaching and Learning Literature, Journal of Children's Literature,* and *New Advocate.* The people who taught children's literature courses in English departments frequently mentioned *The Lion and the Unicorn, Children's Literature,* and *Children's Literature Association Quarterly.* Almost everyone I spoke to was surprised to learn that are there are twenty-eight periodicals that deal extensively with children's literature and at least another twenty-three that regularly publish articles on the topic. The findings of my informal survey suggest that the subdivisions within the field of children's literature have had the unfortunate effect of limiting the readership of the numerous journals that deal with children's literature. One of my goals in writing this chapter is to help the members of these various subdivisions to become more familiar with the journals from the other subdivisions.

This chapter provides key information about a wide variety of journals and periodicals that publish articles about children's literature. The first part of the chapter provides descriptions of journals that focus largely on children's literature and supplies subscription information for these journals. The chapter closes with an annotated list of twenty-two other journals that regularly include articles on some aspect of children's literature. All of the journals covered in this chapter are either published in the United States or are widely available in America. This chapter does not include information on journals that focus on just one author. Such journals are usually published by organizations that are devoted to particular authors, and I have made note of these publications in my chapter on organizations related to children's literature. Readers should also be aware that the information I have provided about the costs of subscribing to these journals is always subject to change.

Journals that deal extensively with children's literature

ALAN Review   *ALAN Review* is brought out three times a year by the Assembly on Literature for Adolescents, which is affiliated with the National Council of Teachers of English. This journal publishes a variety of articles, including critical studies of novels for young adults, annotated bibliographies of young adult books that focus on particular themes, and reports on the use of young adult literature in the classroom. It also includes reviews of recently published books for adolescents and a number of regular columns, such as "The Library Connection," The Censorship Connection," and "The Diversity Connection." The annual subscription rate, which includes membership in the Assembly on Literature for Adolescents, is $15.

For subscription information:
ALAN Review
C/O William Subick
National Council of Teachers
   of English
1111 W. Kenyon Rd.
Urbana, IL 61801-1096
(217) 328-3870
Website: http://scholar.lib.
   vt.edu/ejournals/ALAN/
   alan-review. html

Book Links   *Book Links* is a bimonthly magazine published by the American Library Association. As stated in its mission statement, this "magazine is designed for teachers, librarians, library media specialists, booksellers, parents and other adults interested in connecting children with books." *Book Links* regularly publishes bibliographies, interviews with authors and illustrators, essays linking books on a similar theme, and ideas for book discussions and classroom activities. Its special features include a columns titled "Early Books," which highlights selections for preschool children, "EarthBeat," which covers books that deal with environmental issues, and "Dateline USA," which showcases books about American history. The annual subscription rate is $22.

For subscription information:
Book Links
434 W. Downer
Aurora, IL 60506
(630) 892-7465

The Book Report   One of several library periodicals sponsored by Linworth Publishing, *The Book Report* is intended for junior and senior high school librarians. It comes out bimonthly during the school year. It regularly publishes profiles of authors of young adult fiction, articles on how school librarians can encourage the use of literature in their schools' curricula, and reviews of novels and works of nonfiction for young adults. The annual subscription rate is $39.

For subscription information:
The Book Report
Subscription Department
Linworth Publishing
480 E. Wilson Bridge Rd., Ste. L
Worthington, OH 43085-2372
(614) 436-7107
email: newslin@aol.com

Bookbird   Published quarterly by the International Board of Books for Young People, *Bookbird* covers many facets of international children's literature. It regularly publishes profiles of children's authors and illustrators, news about international events related to children's literature, and surveys of children's literature from various countries. Many of its issues are based on themes. Examples of recent themes include Postcolonial Children's Literature, Girls and Women, and Philosophy for Children. The International Board of Books for Young People also sponsors the Hans Christian Andersen Awards. Shortly after the announcement of the winners of this award, *Bookbird* devotes an issue to profiling the winners as well as the nominees. Annual subscription rates are $30 for individuals and $40 for institutions.

For subscription information:
Bookbird Subscriptions
P.O. Box 807
Highland Park, IL 60035-0807

The Bulletin of the Center for Children's Books   Founded in 1945, *The Bulletin of the Center for Children's Books* is one of the nation's oldest and most respected children's book review journals for librarians. It is published monthly (except

For subscription information:
*The Bulletin of the Center for
   Children's Books*
Subscription Department
University of Illinois Press
1325 South Oak St.
Champaign, IL 61820
(217) 333-8935
Website: http://edfu.lis.uiuc.
   edu/puboff/bccb

for August) by the University of Illinois Press in cooperation with the University of Illinois Graduate School of Library and Information Science. Each issue contains about 75 concise summaries and critical evaluations of recently published books for children or young adults. At the end of each issue is a section called "Professional Connections: Resources for Teachers and Librarians," featuring reviews of books about children's literature. Annual subscription rates are $35 for individuals and $40 for institutions.

Canadian Children's Literature *Canadian Children's Literature* is a scholarly journal that comes out four times a year. Its articles and reviews are either in English or French, and its emphasis is primarily on Canadian children's books and their authors. Many of its issues are theme based. A recent issue, for example, focused on the macabre in children's literature. The annual subscription rates for readers from the United States are $39 for individuals and $43 for institutions.

For subscription information:
Canadian Children's Literature
Departments of English and
    French
University of Guelph
Guelph, Ontario N1G 2W1
(519) 824-4120, ext. 3189

Children's Book Review Magazine This slickly produced magazine is published on a quarterly basis by Grove Communications. Intended primarily for parents, *Children's Book Review Magazine* publishes reviews of a wide variety of children's books, including picture books, novels, collections of poetry, and works of nonfiction. Each issue also includes material about selected authors and illustrators. The Winter 1996 issue, for example, featured interviews with Julius Lester and Petra Mathers and a profile of Avi. The annual subscription rate is $12.90.

For subscription information:
Children's Book Review Magazine
P.O. Box 5082
Brentwood, TN 37024-5082
(800) 543-7220

Children's Literature *Children's Literature* is an annual journal sponsored by the Children's Literature Association and the Modern Language Association Division on Children's Literature and published by Yale University Press. One of the most scholarly journals in the field, *Children's Literature* publishes lengthy and well-researched analyses of classic children's novels and other critically acclaimed children's books. It also publishes numerous reviews of books about children's literature. At the end of each issue is a section titled "Dissertations of Note," which provides abstracts of recently written dissertations that deal with children's literature. In order to subscribe to this journal, one must join the Children's Literature Association. Information about joining the Children's Literature Association can be found in chapter 4 of this book. However, individual issues of *Children's Literature* can be purchased directly from Yale University Press for $16 per paperback issue, plus a $3.50 shipping charge.

For information about purchasing individual issues:
Yale University Press
P.O. Box 209040
New Haven, CT 06520-9040

Children's Literature Association Quarterly An official organ of the Children's Literature Association, the *Children's Literature Association Quarterly* publishes scholarly articles, reviews of books about children's literature, and news related to the Association's activities. Usually, the issues focus on special topics. Recent examples include "Ecology and the Child," "Critical Theory and Adolescent Literature," and "Children's Literature and the New Historicism." In order to subscribe to this journal, one must join the Children's Literature Association.

For information about joining the association see chapter 4, or contact:
Children's Literature Assn.
P.O. Box 138
Battle Creek, MI 49016
(616) 965-8180
email: chla@mic.lib.mi.us

Children's Literature in Education   Published quarterly by the Human Sciences Press, *Children's Literature in Education* is an international journal with editorial offices in both North America and the United Kingdom. It publishes critical evaluations of individual authors or single works, pedagogical articles related to the use of children's literature in the classroom, and examinations of the reading process and its role in childhood and adolescence. It also occasionally includes reviews of professional or scholarly books about children's literature. Annual subscription rates are $32 for individuals and $135 for institutions.

For subscription information:
Subscription Department
Human Sciences Press
233 Spring Street
New York, NY 10013-1578
(212) 620-8468

The Dragon Lode   *The Dragon Lode* is published three times a year by the Children's Literature and Reading Special Interest Group of the International Reading Association. Intended primarily for teachers, it includes articles on incorporating children's literature in the elementary school curriculum, information about authors, reviews of children's books, and annotated bibliographies of children's books that relate to particular themes. It is possible to subscribe to *Dragon Lode* without joining its sponsoring organization. The annual subscription rate is $10.

For subscription information:
IRA Children's Literature
     and Reading SIG
C/O Laura Robb
444 Fairmont Ave.
Winchester, VA 22601

Emergency Librarian   Described in its promotional literature as a "magazine for school library professionals," *Emergency Librarian* is published five times a year. It has offices in both Canada and the United States, and it covers material from both countries in its articles and book reviews. While many of its feature articles deal with issues related to library services, it often publishes articles that relate directly to children's literature. Recent examples include an article on the portrayal of parents in contemporary children's books and an article on recent changes in the children's book publishing industry. *Emergency Librarian* also runs several regular columns that focus on children's literature, including "Books for Children," "Books for Young Adults," and "Portraits," which is actually a series of interviews with children's authors. The annual subscription rate is $44.

For subscription information:
Emergency Librarian
Box 34069, Dept. 284
Seattle, WA 98124-1069
(604) 925-0266

The Five Owls   *The Five Owls*, which is published five times a year by the Hamline University Graduate School, is intended for librarians, educators, book collectors and other readers who are seriously interested in children's literature. Each issue is focused on a theme, such as Australian children's books or holidays and festivals. Usually the cover story and several other articles relate to the theme of the particular issue. Also contained in each issue is a section titled "New Books of Merit," which features reviews of recently published children's books. The annual subscription rate is $20.

For subscription information:
The Five Owls
     Crossroads Center
MS-C1924
1536 Hewitt Ave.
Hamline University
St. Paul, MN 55104
(612) 644-7377
email: fiveowls@seq.hamline.edu
Website: http://www.hamline.edu/depts/gradprog/5owls

The Horn Book Magazine   Founded in 1924, *Horn Book* is the oldest children's literature journal in the United States. It is published six times a year, and it features a wide variety of articles and numerous reviews of books for children and adolescents. It also publishes the acceptance speeches delivered by the winners of both the Caldecott and Newbery awards. At the back of each issue is a section titled "The Hunt Breakfast," which includes announcements of awards, conferences, and other items of interest to the children's

For subscription information:
The Horn Book Magazine
11 Beacon St.
Boston, MA 02108
(617) 227-1555
email: magazine@hbook,com

book world. Annual subscription rates are $36 for individuals and $43 for institutions.

Journal of Children's Literature   Published twice annually, the *Journal of Children's Literature* is sponsored by the Children's Literature Assembly of the National Council of Teachers of English. It publishes a wide variety of articles related to children's literature, including critical studies of individual authors or titles, discussions of teaching strategies involving the use of children's literature, and analyses of children's responses to works of literature. Some of the issues revolve around themes. The Spring 1997 issue, for example, features articles that address the topic of "Teachers as Readers of Literature." The annual subscription rate, which includes membership in the Children's Literature Assembly, is $20.

For subscription information:
Children's Literature Assembly
C/O Marjorie R. Hancock
2037 Plymouth Rd.
Manhattan, KS 66502

Journal of Youth Services in Libraries   *Journal of Youth Services in Libraries* is published quarterly by the American Library Association. It is the official organ of the Association for Library Services to Children (ALSC) and the Young Adult Library Services Association (YALSA), both of which are divisions of the American Library Association. Although this journal does not focus entirely on children's literature, it regularly publishes interviews with children's authors, articles about improving children's access to works of literature, and reviews of books about children's literature. It also publishes the acceptance speeches delivered by the winners of both the Caldecott and Newbery awards. For members of ALSC or YALSA, the subscription cost is included in their membership fees. Information about joining these organizations can be found in chapter 4 of this book. The annual subscription rate for readers who do not belong to ALSC or YALSA is $40.

For subscription information:
Journal of Youth Services in Libraries
American Library Association
50 E. Huron St.
Chicago, IL 60611
(800) 545-2433

The Kobrin Letter   *The Kobrin Letter*, as its title suggests, is a newsletter, not a journal, but it contains information that is difficult to find in longer periodicals. It specializes in nonfiction for children, which is an aspect of children's literature that is often ignored by many children's literature journals. The six issues that come out each year feature capsule reviews of recently published books for children. These reviews are organized around themes. The September 1996 issue, for example, features a series of reviews of books that deal with castles and knights. The annual subscription rate is $12.

For subscription information:
The Kobrin Letter
732 Greer Road
Palo Alto, California 94303
(415) 856-6658

Language Arts   One of the major journals sponsored by the National Council of Teachers of English (NCTE), *Language Arts* is published eight times a year. As is stated in the front of each issue, this journal covers "all facets of language arts learning and teaching, focusing primarily on issues concerning children of preschool through middle school age." Although it does not focus entirely on children's literature, it regularly includes articles about the use of children's books in the elementary school curriculum. Each October, it runs a list of children's books that the editors consider to be especially notable. Annual subscriptions rates, which include membership in NCTE, are $40 for individuals and $50 for institutions.

For subscription information:
Language Arts
National Council of Teachers of English
1111 W. Kenyon Road
Urbana, Illinois 61801-1096
(217) 328-3870

Library Talk   *Library Talk* is a sister journal to *Book Report*. Both are brought out by Linworth Publishing, and both are intended for school librarians. The main difference between the two is that *Library Talk* is for elementary school librarians and *Book Report* is for librarians working in junior and senior high schools. Published five times during the school year, *Library Talk* features articles about children's authors and illustrators, tips on library programs and activities involving children's literature, reviews of recently published children's books, and a column about multicultural children's books. The annual subscription rate is $39.

For subscription information:
Library Talk
Subscription Department
Linworth Publishing
480 E. Wilson Bridge Rd., Ste. L
Worthington, OH 43085-2372
(614) 436-7107
email: newslin@aol.com

The Lion and the Unicorn   This scholarly journal is published by the Johns Hopkins University Press. Each year it brings out one general issue and two thematic issues. Themes of recent issues include "*Struwwelpeter* and Classical Children's Literature" and "Irish Children's Literature." The general issue always features an essay on a "forgotten" children's author. Each issue also includes numerous review essays on important publications and scholarship dealing with children's culture. The annual subscription rates are $21 for individuals and $41 for institutions.

For subscription information:
Johns Hopkins University
    Press
Journals Division
2715 North Charles St.
Baltimore, MD 21218-4319
(410) 516-6987

The Mailbox Bookbag   The Education Center, the publisher of the *Mailbox Bookbag*, describes this magazine as "the teacher's idea magazine for children's literature." Intended for kindergarten through third-grade teachers, *Mailbox Bookbag* features short reviews of recent children's books, annotated bibliographies of books that teachers can use in thematic literature units, and tips sent in by readers on how they incorporate children's literature in their teaching plans. *Mailbox Bookbag* comes out four times a year. The annual subscription rate is $29.95.

For subscription information:
The Mailbox Bookbag
The Education Center
P.O. Box 9753
Greensboro, NC 27429-0753
(910) 273-9409

MultiCultural Review   *MultiCultural Review* is published quarterly by the Greenwood Publishing Group. Although it does not focus entirely on children's literature, it regularly includes articles about books for children and young adults. Some recent examples of such articles include an analysis of books about Latinos for children, a survey of Puerto Rican children's literature, and an interview with an African American writer and educator in which he discusses his approach to teaching *Huckleberry Finn* in the public schools. It also publishes reviews of children's books and curricular materials. Annual subscription rates are $29.95 for individuals and $59 for institutions.

For subscription information:
MultiCultural Review
Greenwood Publishing Group
88 Post Road West
P.O. Box 5007
Westport, CT 06881-5007
(203) 226-3571

The New Advocate   *The New Advocate*, a quarterly journal sponsored by Christopher-Gordon Publishers, has emerged as a central organ for the literature-based teaching movement. Each issue is divided into four sections: "The Creative Process," which features articles by and about children's authors and illustrators; "Concepts and Themes," which consists of research reports and theoretical studies; "Practical Reflections," which features articles that provide practical information on how to use children's literature in the classroom; and "Children's Voices: Responding to Literature," which publishes children's essays and journal entries about their responses to books that they have read. Each issue also includes a column titled "Connecting Readers and

For subscription information:
The New Advocate
Christopher-Gordon Publishers
480 Washington St.
Norwood, MA 02062
(617) 762-5577

Writers with Books" and another column titled "Connecting Educators with Professional Resources." The annual subscription rate is $30.

Parents' Choice   Published four times a year by the Parents' Choice Foundation, *Parents' Choice* describes itself as a "non-profit guide to all the media for children." Each issue features reviews of children's books. Also featured, however, are reviews of computer programs, magazines, television programs, home video releases, and toys. Among the people who write for *Parents' Choice* or serve on its advisory board are some very prominent figures in the field of children's literature, including the authors Julius Lester, Jane Yolen, and Bette Greene, and such critics as Selma Lanes, John Cech, and Peter Neumeyer. The annual subscription rate is $20.

For subscription information:
Parents' Choice Foundation
P.O. Box 185
Newton, MA 02168
(617) 965-5913
email: parchoice@aol.com

School Library Journal   Published monthly, *School Library Journal* is one of only a few periodicals that reviews a significant percentage of the new books for children and young adults that are released each year. It also publishes interviews with children's authors, general interest articles that deal with children's books, articles about the operation of school libraries, and news about awards and special events related to children's literature. The annual subscription rate is $79.50.

For subscription information:
School Library Journal
P.O. Box 57559
Boulder, CO 80322-7559
(800) 456-9409

Signal   *Signal* is the leading children's literature journal from Great Britain. Published three times a year by the Thimble Press, *Signal* features scholarly articles about children's books and discussions of literary criticism as it relates to children's literature. *Signal* focuses primarily on British and Irish children's literature, but it occasionally publishes articles that deal with children's books from the United States or Canada. The annual subscription rate for readers from the United States is $27.

For subscription information:
The Thimble Press
Lockwood, Station Rd.
Woodchester, Stroud
Glos. GL5 5EQ
United Kingdom

Teaching and Learning Literature   *Teaching and Learning Literature* is published five times a year by Essmont Publishing. Dedicated to forging links between teachers and scholars, this journal includes pedagogical articles that deal with literature-based reading programs as well as reflective essays on the history and nature of children's literature. *Teaching and Learning Literature* also publishes reviews of children's books and lengthy review essays on important works about children's literature. The annual subscription rates are $34.95 for individuals and $60 for institutions. A special subscription rate of $22 is available to students.

For subscription information:
Teaching and Learning Literature
Essmont Publishing
P.O. Box 186
Brandon, VT 05733-0186
(802) 247-3488

Voice of Youth Advocates   *Voice of Youth Advocates*, generally known as *VOYA*, is intended for librarians who serve young adults. Published bimonthly by Scarecrow Press, *VOYA* includes articles about young adult literature as well as numerous book reviews. The reviews are grouped in the following categories: fiction; science fiction, fantasy and horror; nonfiction; professional; and reference. The annual subscription rate is $38.50.

For subscription information:
VOYA
Scarecrow Press
4720 Boston Way
Lanham, MD 20706
(301) 459-3366

Journalsthatregularlypublisharticlesaboutchildren'sliterature

Appraisal: Science Books for Young People   Publishes reviews of children's books that deal with science. (605 Commonwealth Ave., Boston, MA 02215)

Booklist   Publishes reviews of new books for children and young adults. (50 E. Huron St., Chicago, IL 60611)

Children's Folklore Review   Occasionally publishes articles about children's books that are tied to folklore. (East Carolina University, English Department, Greenville, NC 27834)

Elementary School Journal   Occasionally publishes articles about the use of children's literature in the elementary school curriculum. (5720 S. Woodlawn Ave., Chicago, IL 60637)

English Journal   Occasionally publishes articles about the use of young adult literature in the secondary school curriculum. (1111 W. Kenyon Rd., Urbana, IL 61801)

Home Education Magazine   Occasionally publishes articles on the relationship between children's literature and home schooling. (Box 1083, Tonasket, WA 98855)

Journal of American Culture   Occasionally publishes articles about American children's literature. (Bowling Green State University, Bowling Green, OH 43403)

Journal of Popular Culture   Often publishes articles about comic books, series books, and other forms of children's popular culture. (Bowling Green State University, Bowling Green, OH 43403)

Journal of Reading   Publishes articles on the use of young adult literature in the teaching of reading to adolescents. (800 Barksdale Rd., Box 8139, Newark, DE 19714)

Journal of Reading Behavior   Occasionally publishes articles on children's literature as it relates to the issue of literacy. (11 E. Hubbard, Ste. 200, Chicago, IL 60611)

Journal of the Fantastic in the Arts   Occasionally publishes articles on fantasy children's books. (Florida Atlantic University, Boca Raton, FL 33431)

Mythlore   Occasionally publishes articles on fantasy children's books. (1008 N. Monterey St., Alhambra, CA 91801)

Primary Voices K-6   Occasionally publishes articles on the use of children's literature in the elementary school curriculum. (1111 Kenyon Rd., Urbana, IL 61801)

Reading Horizons   Occasionally publishes articles about children's literature as it relates to the teaching of reading. (Western Michigan University, Kalamazoo, MI 49008)

Reading Improvement   Occasionally publishes articles about children's literature as it relates to the teaching of remedial reading. (Box 8508, Spring Hill Sta., Mobile, AL 36608)

Reading Research and Instruction   Occasionally publishes articles about children's literature as it relates to the teaching of reading. (Pittsburg State University, Pittsburg, KS 66762)

Reading Teacher   Occasionally publishes articles about children's literature as it relates to the teaching of reading. (800 Barksdale Rd., Box 8139, Newark, DE 19714)

School Library Media Quarterly   Occasionally publishes articles about children's literature as it relates to the operation of school libraries and media centers. (50 E. Huron St., Chicago, IL 60611)

Science and Children   Occasionally publishes articles about the use of children's literature in the teaching of science. (1742 Connecticut Ave. NW, Washington, DC 20009)

Social Education   Occasionally publishes articles about the use of children's literature in the teaching of social studies. (3501 Newark St. NW, Washington, DC 20016)

Storytelling Magazine   Publishes articles about the use of children's literature in storytelling programs. (P.O. Box 309, Jonesborough, TN 37659)

Teaching K–8   Occasionally publishes articles about the use of children's literature in the elementary school curriculum. (40 Richards Ave., Norwalk, CT 06854)

Voices from the Middle   Occasionally publishes articles about the use of children's literature in the middle school curriculum. (National Council of Teachers of English, 1111 Kenyon Rd., Urbana, IL 61801)

Young Children   Occasionally publishes articles about the use of picture books in programs for preschoolers. (1509 16th St., NW, Washington, DC 20036)

The Good Boy's Soliloquy. Published by Samuel Wood & Sons, New York, 1822.

Organizations Related to Children's Literature

Chapter 4

There is an abundance of organizations that relate in one way or another to the field of children's literature. Some of these organizations, such as the Children's Literature Association, promote the scholarly study of children's literature. Others, such as the Association for Library Service to Children, focus on the concerns of professionals who deal with children's literature as part of their work. A number of organizations, such as the International Wizard of Oz Club, appeal to admirers of particular children's authors or specific types of children's books.

All these various organizations offer their members numerous benefits and opportunities. Most of them produce publications, ranging from newsletters to scholarly journals. Many of them also hold conferences and meetings during which their members can listen to lectures and talks or deliver presentations to interested audiences. Some of these organizations sponsor awards and scholarships that their members may be eligible to receive. Still other organizations provide their members with access to special research facilities or library collections. Perhaps the greatest benefit of belonging to any of these organizations is the pleasure and stimulation that comes from associating with people who share one's special interests and concerns.

What follows are descriptions of 29 organizations that relate to children's literature. The first organizations that I have listed promote the scholarly study of children's literature. The next section deals with organizations that serve the people who work in certain professions, such as librarians or reading teachers. The final section deals with organizations that are devoted to the study and appreciation of particular authors or types of children's literature. Readers should be aware, however, that there are some organizations that do not fit neatly into just one of these three areas. Some professional organizations, for instance, also promote scholarly research related to children's literature. I have provided membership information for each organization, but it is important to remember that membership dues and the addresses of contact people are always subject to change.

Scholarly organizations

CHILDREN'S LITERATURE ASSOCIATION   Founded in 1973, the Children's Literature Association now has approximately 750 members. Most of the membership comes from the United States and Canada, but there also members from Great Britain, Germany, France, Sweden, Japan, India, Australia, and a number of other countries. As stated in its membership brochure, the Association's goals are "to encourage serious scholarship and research in children's literature, to enhance the professional stature of the graduate and undergraduate teaching of children's literature, and to encourage high standards of criticism in children's literature."

The Association helps sponsor two scholarly publications—the *Children's Literature Association Quarterly* and an annual journal titled *Children's Literature*. Each year the Association holds a major conference, featuring keynote presentations by prominent children's authors and important literary critics and many concurrent sessions during which participants present scholarly papers. It also gives several annual awards, including the Phoenix Award, which recognizes an outstanding children's book that was published twenty years earlier but did not receive a major award at the time of publication, and an award for an outstanding book of criticism or history in the field of children's literature.

Annual membership dues for people living in the United States are $65 for regular members, $40 for retired members, and $30 for student members.

For more information:
Children's Literature Assn.
P.O. Box 138
Battle Creek, MI 49016
(616) 965-8180

INTERNATIONAL RESEARCH SOCIETY FOR CHILDREN'S LITERATURE   Founded in 1970 by seven children's literature specialists from five different countries, the International Research Society for Children's Literature now has approximately 250 members from about 40 countries. The aims of the Society are to promote research and scholarship in children's and youth literature and to facilitate cooperation and the exchange of information among researchers in different countries.

Every other year the Society organizes a congress around a particular theme. Past themes have included the portrayal of the child in children's literature; multiculturalism in children's literature; and the literary aspects of fantasy for children and young people. The Society also sponsors publications, a research grant given to a new scholar in the field, and an award recognizing an outstanding scholarly book about children's literature.

Scholars interested in joining the Society must apply for membership. Evidence of active engagement in children's literature research is essential for acceptance into the Society. Annual membership dues are $30.

For more information:
Carole A. Scott
Secretary, IRSCL
Division of Undergraduate
    Studies
San Diego State University
San Diego, CA 92182-0418
(619) 594-1261

CHILDREN'S FOLKLORE SECTION OF THE AMERICAN FOLKLORE SOCIETY   Organized in the fall of 1977, the Children's Folklore Section of the American Folklore Society consists of approximately two hundred scholars who are interested in the various forms of children's traditional culture, including stories, songs, rhymes, games, and toys. Twice a year this organization publishes the *Children's Folklore Review*. It also sponsors several panels and forums during the annual meeting of the American Folklore Society.

Many of the members of this organization have a strong interest in the con-

For more information:
Dr. Danielle Roemer
CFS Treasurer
Department of Literature and
    Language
Northern Kentucky University
Highland Heights, KY 41099-
    1500

nections between folklore and children's literature. Articles published in *Children's Folklore Review* and presentations given during the organization's annual meeting often focus on this topic. The organization's Aesop Prize, which it awards each year, goes to an excellent children's book that is based on folklore.

Annual membership dues for people living in the United States are $10. This organization is affiliated with the American Folklore Society but does not require its members to join the parent organization.

INTERNATIONAL ASSOCIATION FOR THE FANTASTIC IN THE ARTS Since its inception in the late 1970s, the International Association for the Fantastic in the Arts has promoted the scholarly study of all types of fantasy literature as well as films, television programs and other art forms that make use of fantasy elements. Among its approximately 325 members are literary critics, fantasy authors, film critics, art historians, and folklorists. Although the Association does not focus exclusively on children's literature, it includes within its scope all children's books that can be classified as works of fantasy or science fiction.

In March of every year, the Association holds its International Conference on the Fantastic in the Arts. This conference always takes place in Ft. Lauderdale, Florida. Prominent children's authors are often included among the conference's special guests, and there are always presentations given that deal with children's literature. In addition to sponsoring this conference, the Association publishes the *Journal of the Fantastic in the Arts*.

Annual membership dues for people living in the United States are $50.

For more information:
Martha Bartter
IAFA Treasurer
Language and Literature
Truman State University
Kirksville, MO 63501
Website: http://ebbs.english.
   vt.edu/iafa.home/

POPULAR CULTURE ASSOCIATION When Ray Browne founded the Popular Culture Association in 1969, it consisted of a small group of scholars who were interested primarily in popular literature. It has since grown into a 3,500-member organization that encompasses all forms of culture intended for mass audiences. The Association publishes numerous journals, including the *Journal of Popular Culture*, the *Journal of American Culture*, and the *Journal of Cultural Geography*. It also sponsors a large conference each spring, publishes many scholarly books, and supports a library of popular literature located on the campus of Bowling Green State University in Bowling Green, Ohio.

The members of the Popular Culture Association often conduct research related to children's literature. During the Association's annual conference, there are usually presentations on children's series books, dime novels, comic books, and film versions of children's novels. Similarly, articles on these topics can frequently be found in both the *Journal of Popular Culture* and the *Journal of American Culture*.

Annual membership dues for people living in the United States are $45.

For more information:
Popular Culture Association
Bowling Green State Univ.
Popular Culture Center
Bowling Green, OH 43403
(419) 372-7861

Professional organizations

CHILDREN'S LITERATURE ASSEMBLY OF THE NATIONAL COUNCIL OF TEACHERS OF ENGLISH The Children's Literature Assembly of the NCTE was organized in the mid-1970s in order to provide a forum for teachers interested in using children's literature in the classroom. In more recent years, its membership has expanded to include librarians, children's authors, and publishers, but most of

For more information:
Children's Literature Assembly
C/O Marjorie R. Hancock
2037 Plymouth Road
Manhattan, KS 66503

the members are educators who teach children's literature either to children or to college students. The Assembly currently has about 525 members.

The Assembly publishes the *Journal of Children's Literature*, which comes out twice a year. The Assembly also prepares and publicizes its annual list of Notable Children's Books in the Language Arts. Every November, the Assembly sponsors a series of events during NCTE's fall convention, including a special breakfast with a noted children's author.

Annual membership dues for people living in the United States are $20 for regular members and $10 for student members. The Assembly is affiliated with the National Council of Teachers of English but does not require its members to join the parent organization.

ASSEMBLY ON LITERATURE FOR ADOLESCENTS OF THE NATIONAL COUNCIL OF TEACHERS OF ENGLISH   Formed in 1973, the Assembly on Literature for Adolescents began as a small group of mostly secondary school teachers of English, but it quickly grew into 2,000-member organization. The current membership consists of public school teachers who work with adolescents, scholars who research and teach about young adult books, librarians who deal with adolescents either in the schools or in public libraries, and publishers who specialize in young adult literature.

For more information:
ALAN Membership Office
National Council of Teachers of English
1111 W. Kenyon Rd.
Urbana, IL 61801-1096
(217) 328-3870
Website: http://english.byu.edu/alan.htm

The Assembly publishes the *ALAN Review*, which comes out three times a year. Each year the Assembly presents the ALAN Award to a person who has over the course of his or her career made a lasting contribution to the field of adolescent literature. Every November, the Assembly sponsors a series of events during NCTE's fall conference, including a special breakfast with a noted author of books for young adults. Immediately after convention, the Assembly sponsors a two-day workshop during which authors, teachers, and scholars discuss a particular theme related to adolescent literature.

The annual membership dues for people living in the United States are $15. The Assembly is affiliated with the National Council of Teachers of English but does not require its members to join the parent organization.

INTERNATIONAL READING ASSOCIATION   Since its founding in 1956, the International Reading Association has been devoted to promoting literacy and improving the quality of reading instruction. It is a very large organization with a membership of over 92,000 from nearly one hundred countries. It publishes numerous books and several journals, including *The Reading Teacher* and the *Journal of Adolescent and Adult Literacy*. In addition to holding an annual convention in the spring, the International Reading Association regularly sponsors several regional conferences.

For more information:
International Reading Assn.
800 Barksdale Rd.
P.O. Box 8139
Newark, DE 19714-8139
(302) 731-1600

Members of the International Reading Association who are especially interested in children's literature should consider joining two of the special interest groups sponsored by the Association. One of these groups, called Children's Literature and Reading, promotes creative uses of children's books in literacy programs. The other, called Network on Adolescent Literature, provides its members with opportunities to discuss adolescent literature with colleagues. It also supplies members with instructional techniques on using adolescent literature in the classroom. Information on how to join these groups can be obtained from the central office of the Association.

The annual membership dues for people living in the United States are $30 for regular members and $18 for student members.

COLLEGE READING ASSOCIATION   The College Reading Association began around 1960 as a loosely organized group of developmental reading specialists from colleges and universities. The Association was formally incorporated in 1963, and it now has approximately 470 members, most of whom teach college-level courses on literacy and reading instruction. The Association is organized into the four following divisions: Teacher Education, Clinical, College Reading, and Adult Learning. The Association publishes the journal *Reading Research and Instruction*, and it holds an annual conference at the end of October or the beginning of November.

Of the Association's four divisions, the Teacher Education Division has the most connections to children's literature. The members of this division are especially interested in conducting research into how children's literature can effectively be used to teach reading and writing skills to children. The findings of this research are often presented at the Association's conference or published in *Reading Research and Instruction*.

Annual membership dues for people living in the United States are $60 for regular members and $30 for student members.

For more information:
Dr. Gary L. Shaffer
Business Manager
College Reading Association
James Madison University
83 Sharon St.
Harrisonburg, VA 22801-2715
(540) 434-2951

ASSOCIATION FOR LIBRARY SERVICE TO CHILDREN   The Association for Library Service to Children (ALSC) can trace its origins back to the formation, in 1900, of the Section for Children's Librarians of the American Library Association. In 1941, this initial group became the American Library Association, Division of Libraries for Children and Young Adults. In 1957, this group was divided into two groups: the Children's Services Division and the Young Adult Services Division. In the mid-1970s, the Children's Services Division was renamed the Association for Library Service to Children. ALSC now has 4,000 members, making it the largest organization of its kind in the entire world. Throughout its long and complicated history, ALSC has remained dedicated to supporting and improving library services to children as well as supporting the profession of children's librarianship.

ALSC's specific activities and projects include the sponsorship of institutes and training programs for children's librarians, the publication of materials designed to be used by librarians and media specialists, and the administration of the Newbery Medal, the Caldecott Medal, the Laura Ingalls Wilder Award and several other awards related to children's literature. Also, ALSC, together with the Young Adult Library Services Association, publishes the *Journal of Youth Services in Libraries*.

Annual membership dues for regular members are $45. However, since the Association is an official division of the American Library Association, members must also join the parent organization, which costs $95 per year. Thus, regular membership dues come to a total of $140. The regular membership is only one of a number membership categories. The dues for first-year members, second-year members, student members, and retired members are all less than the regular dues.

For more information:
Association for Library Service
    to Children
American Library Association
50 East Huron Street
Chicago, IL 60611
(800) 545-2433, ext. 2163
Website: http://www.ala.org/
    alsc.html

YOUNG ADULT LIBRARY SERVICES ASSOCIATION The Young Adult Library Services Association (YALSA) was established in 1957 under the name Young Adult Services Division of the American Library Association. Since 1991, it has been known by its current name. It remains, however, an official division of the American Library Association. YALSA is now a 2,000-member organization. Its basic goal, as stated in its membership brochure is "to advocate, promote and strengthen service to young adults (ages 12–18) as part of the continuum of total library services."

YALSA-specific activities and projects include the sponsorship of training programs for young adult librarians, the publication of materials designed to be used by librarians and media specialists, the compilation and distribution of an annual list of Best Books for Young Adults, and the granting of the Margaret A. Edwards Award, which goes to a living author who has made a lasting contribution to young adult literature. Also, YALSA, together with the Association for Library Service to Children, publishes the *Journal of Youth Services in Libraries.*

Annual membership dues for regular members are $40. However, since YALSA is an official division of the American Library Association, members must also join the parent organization, which costs $95 per year. Thus, regular membership dues come to a total of $135. The dues for first-year members and student members are less than the regular dues.

For more information:
Young Adult Library Services
    Association
American Library Association
50 East Huron St.
Chicago, IL 60611
(800) 545-2433, ext. 2433
Website: http://www.ala.org/
    yalsa.html

AMERICAN ASSOCIATION OF SCHOOL LIBRARIANS Founded in 1951, the American Association of School Librarians (AASL) now has approximately 7,600 members, most of whom are elementary or secondary school media specialists. As an official division of the American Library Association, AASL sponsors many sessions at ALA's annual conference. Since the late 1980s, AASL has also held its own conference. One of AASL's other main projects is the publication of the *School Library Media Quarterly.*

Although many of AASL's activities relate only tangentially to children's literature, AASL plays an important role in facilitating the use of children's literature in the schools. It does this by sponsoring reading incentive programs for school children, sponsoring workshops on incorporating children's literature in teachers' and school librarians' curricular plans, and occasionally publishing articles related to children's literature in the *School Library Media Quarterly.*

Annual membership dues for regular members are $40. However, since the Association is an official division of the American Library Association, members must also join the parent organization, which costs $95 per year. Thus, regular membership dues come to a total of $135. The regular membership is only one of a number of membership categories. The dues for first-year members, second-year members, student members, and retired members are all less than the regular dues.

For more information:
American Association of
    School Librarians
American Library Association
50 East Huron St.
Chicago, IL 60611
(800) 545-2433, ext. 4386
Website: http://www.ala.org/
    aasl/index.html

SOCIETY OF CHILDREN'S BOOK WRITERS AND ILLUSTRATORS Formed in 1968, the Society of Children's Book Writers and Illustrators began as a small group of children's authors from the Los Angeles area. It is now an international organization with over 10,000 members. The Society serves as a consolidated

For more information:
Society of Children's Book
    Writers and Illustrators
22736 Vanowen St., Ste. 106
West Hills, CA 91307
(818) 888-8760

voice for professional writers and illustrators. Over the years, it has spoken out on such issues as copyright legislation and the negotiation of contracts between publishers and authors. It also furthers its members' careers by providing them with professional advice and useful information.

The Society is involved in many ongoing projects and activities related to children's literature. Each August it sponsors a national conference during which participants can gain insights into writing and illustrating for children. It also holds regional meetings and workshops, provides several financial grants to help members complete projects, and presents the Golden Kite Awards to outstanding children's books written and/or illustrated by Society members.

The annual membership dues for people living in the United States are $50. Full membership is open to those whose work for children has been published. Associate membership is open to all those with an interest in children's literature, whether or not they have been published. The annual dues are the same for both full and associate memberships.

CHILDREN'S BOOK COUNCIL   Founded in 1945, the Children's Book Council is a nonprofit trade association of children's book publishers and producers of related literacy materials. Its purpose is to promote the use of children's trade books and to disseminate information about books for young people and about trade book publishing. It currently has approximately 80 members, some of which are publishers while others are imprints (or divisions) of major publishing houses.

For more information:
Children's Book Council, Inc.
568 Broadway, Ste. 404
New York, NY 10012
(212) 966-1990
Website: http://www.cbc-
   books.org

The Children's Book Council is involved in a wide range of activities, including the production of curricular materials related to children's literature, the publication of a biannual newsletter titled *CBC Features*, and the organization and maintenance of an examination library of recent books published by the members of the Council. Perhaps its highest profile project is its sponsorship of the National Children's Book Week, which occurs each November during the week before Thanksgiving.

Membership in the Council is open to all U.S. children's book publishers and producers of related literacy materials. Personal memberships are not available, but interested individuals can be added to the Council's mailing list for a one-time fee of $60.

NATIONAL STORYTELLING ASSOCIATION   In 1973, a group of storytellers and lovers of storytelling held the first National Storytelling Festival in Jonesborough, Tennessee. The festival was such a success that the organizers decided to make it an annual event and to form an organization to help plan future festivals. This led to the founding of the National Association for the Preservation and Perpetuation of Storytelling in 1975. Later renamed the National Storytelling Association, it has grown into a 5,600-member organization. In addition to sponsoring the National Storytelling Festival, the Association also publishes the *Storytelling Magazine* and produces a wide variety of books and audiotapes related to storytelling.

For more information:
National Storytelling Assn.
P.O. Box 309
Jonesborough, TN 37659
(423) 753-2171

Although the National Storytelling Association does not focus entirely on storytelling for children, one of its central missions is to help introduce children to the art of storytelling. Over the years, it has published a number of books that relate to this mission, including *Easy-to-Tell Stories for Young Children* and *Tales as Tools: The Power of Story in the Classroom*. It also regularly sponsors workshops on telling stories to children and helps storytellers find stories in the public domain that work well with young audiences. The annual membership dues for people living in the United States are $40.

Specialized organizations

BETSY-TACY SOCIETY   Formed in 1990, the Betsy-Tacy Society has approximately 1,000 members, all of whom are admirers and/or collectors of Maud Hart Lovelace's Betsy-Tacy Books. The Society publishes the *Journal of the Betsy-Tacy Society*, conducts an ongoing campaign to keep the Betsy-Tacy books in print, and occasionally holds conventions in Mankato, Minnesota, where Lovelace was born and where she set most of the Betsy-Tacy books. The annual membership dues are $10.

For more information:
Michele Blake
Betsy-Tacy Membership
P.O. Box 206
North Easton, MA 02356

GEORGE MACDONALD SOCIETY   The George MacDonald Society was formed in 1981. Initially most of its members were from Great Britain, but its membership now includes many Americans and Canadians. The Society publishes a journal titled *North Wind*. It also supports a research collection of works on and by MacDonald, which is housed at King's College in London. The annual membership dues for Americans are $18.

For more information:
The George MacDonald
   Society
C/O John Joseph Flynn
608 Milan Ave.
S. Pasadena, CA 91030

HORATIO ALGER SOCIETY   Founded in 1961, the Horatio Alger Society currently has approximately 250 members. The purpose of the Society, as stated in its literature, is "to further the philosophy of Horatio Alger, Jr., and to encourage the spirit of Strive and Succeed that for half a century guided Alger's undaunted heroes." The Society publishes a magazine titled *Newsboy*, holds an annual convention (usually on the first weekend in May), and provides useful information to members who are trying to add to their collections of Alger books. The annual membership dues are $20.

For more information:
Horatio Alger Society
C/O Robert Kasper
585 E. St. Andrews Drive
Media, PA 19063

HAPPY HOURS BROTHERHOOD   Organized in 1924, the Happy Hours Brotherhood is a loose federation of readers and collectors of dime novels. It currently has approximately 250 members. The main activity of the Brotherhood is the publication of *Dime Novel Round-Up*. Published six times a year, *Dime Novel Round-Up* is devoted to the collection, preservation and study of dime novels, series books, and pulp magazines. This magazine has been published continuously since 1931. The annual membership/subscription dues are $15.

For more information:
Happy Hours Brotherhood
C/O J. Randolph Cox
P.O. Box 226
Dundas, MN 55019-0226

INTERNATIONAL WIZARD OF OZ CLUB   Founded in 1957, the International Wizard of Oz Club now has approximately 2,500 members. To quote from the Club's membership flyer, the purpose of the Club is "to bring together all those interested in L. Frank Baum and Oz." The Club publishes a magazine called *The Baum Bugle*, which comes out three times each year. It also publishes *Oziana*, which is an annual collection of new stories based on the original Oz books, and *The Oz Trading Post*, which is a quarterly newsletter that

For more information:
The International Wizard of
   Oz Club
P.O. Box 266
Kalamazoo, MI 49004-0266

provides information for collectors of Oz books and related memorabilia. Each year the Club sponsors conventions in different areas of the country. The annual membership dues are $15.

LAURA INGALLS WILDER MEMORIAL SOCIETY Formed in 1974, the Laura Ingalls Wilder Memorial Society is based in Pepin, Wisconsin, where Wilder was born and where she set *Little House in the Big Woods*. The Society's 670 members are involved in several projects that celebrate Wilder's connections to Pepin. They acquired part of the original homesite where Wilder spent much of her early childhood and built a replica of the family's log cabin on the spot where the original cabin stood. The Society also operates the Pepin Historical Museum, which houses a collection of artifacts related to Wilder and the time period during which she lived in Pepin. Some of the Society's other projects include the publication of a newsletter and the sponsorship of a two-day festival in Pepin called Laura Ingalls Wilder Days. The annual membership dues are $10.

For more information:
Laura Ingalls Wilder Memorial Society, Inc.
Box 269
Pepin, WI 54759

LEWIS CARROLL SOCIETY OF NORTH AMERICA The Lewis Carroll Society of North America was established in 1974. It meets twice a year at various locations. The Society publishes a newsletter called *Knight Letter* as well as several books and pamphlets related to Carroll. On occasion, the Society organizes expeditions to Carroll sites in Great Britain. Membership dues are $20.

For more information:
Lewis Carroll Society of North America
C/O Ellie Luchinsky
18 Fitzharding Place
Owings Mill, MD 21117
Website: http://www.students.uiuc.edu/~jbirenba/lcsnahp.html

LOUISA MAY ALCOTT MEMORIAL ASSOCIATION Founded in 1911, the Louisa May Alcott Memorial Association is dedicated to preserving the memory of Louisa May Alcott and the other members of the Alcott family. The central activity of the Association is maintaining and operating Orchard House, where the Alcott family lived for many year and where Louisa May Alcott wrote her most famous book, *Little Women*. The Association also publishes a newsletter titled *Alcott Newsnotes*. In the summer, the Association sponsors a series of programs for children. The annual membership dues are $25.

For more information:
Louisa May Alcott Memorial Association
P.O. Box 343
Concord, MA 01742
(598) 369-4118

MARK TWAIN BOYHOOD HOME ASSOCIATES There are a number of organizations that focus on Mark Twain and his writings, but the organization that has the most connections to Twain's writings for children is the Mark Twain Boyhood Home Associates. This organization, which has approximately 700 members, is a branch of the Mark Twain Home Foundation. Established in 1974, the Foundation is responsible for operating and maintaining Twain's boyhood home, a museum that features Twain memorabilia, and several other properties that are associated with Twain's childhood in Hannibal, Missouri. One of the Foundation's other activities in the publication a quarterly newsletter called *The Fence Painter*, which goes to the members of the Mark Twain Boyhood Home Associates. All of the projects sponsored by the Foundation relate to Twain's classic children's book *The Adventures of Tom Sawyer*. The annual membership dues are $10 for individuals and $15 for families.

For more information:
Mark Twain Boyhood Home Associates
208 Hill St.
Hannibal, MO 63401
(573) 221-9010

MYTHOPOEIC SOCIETY Founded in 1967, the Mythopoeic Society is a 700-member organization devoted to the study and appreciation of the works of

J. R. R. Tolkien, C. S. Lewis, and Charles Williams as well as the genres of myth and fantasy. Although the Society does not focus entirely on children's literature, it does include within its scope the children's books by both Tolkien and Lewis. Each summer the Society sponsors a conference. It also publishes three periodicals: *Mythlore,* a quarterly journal featuring scholarly articles and book reviews; *Mythprint,* the Society's monthly newsletter: and *Mythic Circle,* a fantasy fiction magazine that comes out three times a year. The basic annual membership dues are $5, but members who want to receive one or more of the Society's periodicals must pay an additional subscription fee for each periodical that they want sent to them.

For more information:
The Mythopoeic Society
P.O. Box 6707
Altadena, CA 91003
Website: http://home.earth-link.net/~emfarrell/myth-soc/mythsoc.html

NEW YORK C. S. LEWIS SOCIETY   Founded in 1969, the New York C. S. Lewis Society is devoted to increasing the knowledge and understanding Lewis's work, including his books for children. The Society has approximately 550 members, many of whom attend the Society's monthly meetings that are held on the second Friday of the month except August at the Church of Ascension, 12 West 11th Street, in New York City. In addition to holding these meetings, the Society publishes *CSL: The Bulletin of the New York C. S. Lewis Society.* The annual membership dues are $10.

For more information:
New York C. S. Lewis Society
C/O Clara Sarrocco
84-23 77th Ave.
Glendale, NY 11385

RANDOLPH CALDECOTT SOCIETY OF AMERICA   Organized in 1983, the Randolph Caldecott Society of America is based in Saint Augustine, Florida, where Caldecott died in 1886. The Society has approximately one hundred members, many of whom meet twice a year to conduct Society business and to celebrate Caldecott's life and art. The Society's projects include serving as caretaker of Caldecott's grave, supporting the Randolph Caldecott Children's Room at the St. Johns County Library, and providing material about Caldecott to all interested parties. The annual membership dues are $10.

For more information:
Randolph Caldecott Society of America
112 Crooked Tree Trail
Moultrie Trails, R. R. #4
Saint Augustine, FL 32086

SOCIETY OF PHANTOM FRIENDS   Founded in 1985, the Society of Phantom Friends is a 350-member organization that is devoted to the appreciation and collection of series books for girls. The Society's newsletter, *The Whispered Watchword,* is published ten times a year. It contains articles, reviews, and information about girls' series books that are available for purchase. Every year or two, the Society sponsors a convention. The annual membership dues are $26.

For more information:
The Society for Phantom Friends
C/O Kate Emburg
4100 Cornelia Way
North Highlands, CA 95660
(916) 331-7435

UNITED STATES BOARD ON BOOKS FOR YOUNG PEOPLE   The United States Board on Books for Young People is an official section of the International Board on Books for Young People. Established in 1984, the U. S. Board has approximately 400 members. Like its parent organization, the U. S. Board is devoted to promoting international understanding through children's books and to facilitating an international exchange of information concerning children's literature. The U. S. Board publishes a newsletter twice a year, represents the United States at conferences and meetings sponsored by the International Board, and organizes sessions at the annual conventions of sister organizations, such as the American Library Association, the International Reading Association, and the National Council of Teachers of English. The annual membership dues are $25.

For more information:
United States Board on Books for Young People
Secretariat
P. O. Box 8139
Newark, DE 19714-8139

Children's Literature on the Internet

Chapter 5

In the early 1990s, the Internet began to show signs of becoming an important medium for communicating information about children's literature. Many of my colleagues found this development exciting, but as an old-fashioned lover of the printed word, I studiously avoided anything to do with the Internet. Nevertheless, the Internet quickly evolved, and its following grew even faster. Today it provides children's literature specialists with all sorts of resources, diversions, and opportunities to communicate with other people who are interested in children's books.

At the prodding of many colleagues, I finally decided to see what all the fuss was about. I joined a bunch of listservs, spent hours visiting websites, and peppered my computer-literate friends with dozens of questions. While I have certainly not become an expert in these matters, the insights I gleaned from my immersion in cyberspace may be of interest to others who are getting ready to take the plunge.

Through the Internet, children's literature specialists can participate in a variety of listservs that relate to their interests in the field. Listservs are essentially discussion groups that conduct their business via email. The participants in these listservs exchange ideas and information. They often request help on research projects or solicit suggestions related to teaching activities and library programming. In some ways, the exchanges that take place on listservs remind me of the stimulating discussions that occur at conferences during coffee breaks.

Also of interest to children's literature specialists are the hundreds of websites that focus on some aspect of children's literature. These websites are like entries in a zany encyclopedia. They contain all sorts of information in all sorts of formats, and many of them have links to other websites. Each website has its own character. Some are scholarly, some are humorous, and some are just plain weird. There is a free-for-all quality to the world of websites that can be both appealing and annoying.

Some websites contain odd bits of information that would be difficult to find in standard reference works, but users should be aware that not all websites can be fully trusted. Since many websites are the products of individuals working independently, there's no guarantee that information on them has been checked for accuracy by editors or experts in the field. Nevertheless, visiting websites is often an excellent way to begin conducting research on various subjects related to children's literature.

In this chapter, I provide information about both listservs and websites. Each of these has its own electronic address known as a URL, which stands for uniform resource locator. URLs are a string of characters that must be exactly typed. I list the URL for each listserv and website that I discuss, but the distressing truth of the matter is that URLs change fairly often. Fortunately, there are lots of search tools and electronic web guides that can help Internet users locate a listserv or a website without knowing its current URL.

The listservs and websites mentioned in this chapter are just a tiny fraction of what is actually available. The ones I include take fairly general approaches to children's literature and provide ready linkages to the other listservs and websites that deal with specific topics in the field, such as individual authors or particular types of children's books. Elsewhere in this book readers can find the URLs for a number of websites dealing with specific organizations, journals, and library collections.

Listservs

[**Note for subscribing to listservs:** If your email software automatically generates a signature following each message, be certain to type "end" on the line immediately below your request; otherwise the listserv computer may not accept it.]

CHILD_LIT   To quote from the official description of this listserv, Child_lit is "an unmoderated discussion group convened for the express purpose of examining the theory and criticism of literature for children and young adults." Many of its members are professors or graduate students, which perhaps explains why the participants often assume a quasi-academic tone when discussing issues. The membership, however, also includes librarians, children's authors, editors, and publishers. Child_lit owes its origins to Michael Joseph, who is affiliated with Rutgers University Libraries. Joseph, along with the staff members of Rutgers University Computing Services and Rutgers University Libraries, continues to maintain this listserv.

To subscribe:
Send an email message to the following URL: <majordomo@email.rutgers.edu>. Do not include anything in the subject line.
Your message should read "subscribe Child_lit" and close with your email address.

KIDLIT-L   Intended for a somewhat more general audience than Child_lit, KIDLIT-L includes among its members teachers, librarians, college students, parents, and children's authors. The participants often discuss issues related to teaching. One recent exchange, for example, focused on innovative ways to present picture books to children of varying ages. This listserv was founded by Prue Stelling at Binghamton University.

To subscribe:
Send an email message to the following URL: <listserv@bingvmb.cc.binghamton.edu>.
Your message should read "subscribe KIDLIT-L" and close with your first name and last name.

PUBYAC   Most of the members of this listserv are librarians who work with children and young adults. In the words of its official description, PUBYAC is "concerned with the practical aspects of children and young adult services in public libraries, focusing on programming ideas, outreach and literacy programs for children and caregivers, censorship and policy issues, collection development, ... and other pertinent services and issues." This listserv was

To subscribe:
Send an email message to the following URL: <listserv@nysernet.org>.
Your message should read "subscribe PUBYAC" and close with your first name and last name.

founded in 1993 at the University of Pittsburgh's School of Library and Information Science.

CCBC-Net   This listserv is sponsored by the School of Education at the University of Wisconsin-Madison, which also supports the Cooperative Children's Book Center. As is stated in its official description, CCBC-Net provides "opportunities for spontaneous as well as guided discussions of contemporary literature for children and young adults." Each month the subscribers are invited to discuss a subject, which is always announced ahead of time. One month, for example, the subject was Karen Cushman's *The Midwife's Apprentice*. Each of these scheduled discussions is moderated by someone who has a special interest in the subject being discussed.

To subscribe:
Send an email message to the following URL: <listserv@ccbc.soemadfison.wisc.edu>.

Your message should read "subscribe CCBC-Net" and close with your first name and last name.

Websites

THE CHILDREN'S LITERATURE WEB GUIDE   Created and maintained by David K. Brown at the University of Calgary, the Children's Literature Web Guide is the best place to start exploring the myriad websites that deal with children's literature. Brown has gathered together, categorized, and provided access to hundreds of Internet resources related to books for children and young adults. When this website first comes on the screen, a list appears under the heading "More Links." The subheadings on this list include "Authors on the Web," "Resources for Teachers," "Resources for Parents," "Movies and Television Based on Children's Books," and "Children's Publishers and Booksellers." To use this guide, one simply needs to click on the categories that relate to one's specific interests. If one clicks on "Authors on the Web," for example, there will appear on the screen a list of about hundred websites, each of which provides information about individual children's authors or illustrators. To visit one of these websites, one simply needs to click on the author or illustrator's name.

URL:
<http://www.ucalgary.ca/~dkbrown/index.html>

YOUNG ADULT LITERATURE   This website grew out of a graduate course on young adult literature taught at the University of South Florida. Like the Children's Literature Web Guide, Young Adult Literature provides links to many other websites. However, rather than categorize these websites, the creators of Young Adult Literature provide a long list of websites that relate directly or indirectly to literature intended for adolescents. Accompanying each item on this list is a brief annotation describing the website and explaining, if necessary, its connection to young adult literature.

URL:
<http://www.ct.net/~patem/yalit>

VANDERGRIFT'S CHILDREN'S LITERATURE PAGE   This website is one of several created and maintained by Kay E. Vandergrift, a professor at Rutgers University's School of Communication Information and Library Studies. This website is organized into several categories, including "Illustrated Materials for Young Children," "Modern Realistic Fiction," "Fanciful Fiction," and "Poetry." For each of these categories, Vandergrift supplies her own information and insights. She also provides links to other websites that relate to these categories.

URL:
<http://www.scils.rutgers.edu/special/kay/child-lit.html>

VANDERGRIFT'S YOUNG ADULT LITERATURE PAGE   This website is the creation of Kay E. Vandergrift, a professor at Rutgers University's School of Communication Information and Library Studies. Like her website on children's literature, Vandergrift's Young Adult Literature Page is divided into several categories. Two of the most interesting of these are "Young Adult Literature and Reader-Response Criticism" and "Young Adult Literature and Feminist Criticism." Vandergrift is especially interested in these two forms of criticism and provides insights into how they can be applied to young adult literature. For each of the categories covered in Vandergrift's Young Adult Literature Page, there are numerous links to related websites.

URL:
<http://www.scils.rutgers.edu/special/kay/yalit.html>

FAIRROSA CYBER LIBRARY   There is a fanciful quality to this website that takes a little getting used to, but for anyone who is interested in fantasy literature for children, the Fairrosa Cyber Library is well worth visiting. After this website first appears on the screen, one can click on any of the following eight categories: "Reading Room," which features stories and rhymes; "Morwen's Magic Door," which provides links to other websites; "Book Lists;" "Dragons;" "Reviews;" "Articles and Discussions;" and "Lewis Carroll." The section on dragons is especially appealing. It consists of richly annotated lists of children's books about dragons and related subjects.

URL:
<http://www.users.interport/~fairrosa/index.html>

CHILDREN'S BOOK COUNCIL   This website features information about the CBC, as well as a listing of all children's book publishers who are members of the CBC. The list includes links to those member/publishers who have established websites containing information about their publications.

URL:
<http://www.cbcbooks.org>

SOCIETY OF CHILDREN'S BOOK WRITERS AND ILLUSTRATORS   In addition to providing information about the SCBWI, users can use this site to locate information about authors and illustrators who are members of this organization.

URL:
<http://www.scbwi.org>

DEGRUMMOND CHILDREN'S LITERATURE COLLECTION   One of the largest collections of classic children's books is located at the University of Southern Mississippi. Information on the deGrummond Collection and its holdings can be found through its website.

URL:
<http://www.lib.usm.edu/degrumm.htm>

ELECTRONIC RESOURCES FOR YOUTH SERVICES   Links to online reviews of recent children's books and lists of award-winning children's authors.

URL:
<http:www.ccn.cs.dal.ca/~aa331/childlit.html>

NOTES FROM THE WINDOWSILL   Supported primarily by volunteers and through donations, this website offers online reviews of recent children's books.

URL:
<http://www.armory.com/~web/notes.html>

BOOKWIRE   Although this website includes information on adult as well as children's and adult books, it is a useful source of information on children's bookstores and publishers, children's authors on tour, professional conferences, book fairs, as well as *Publishers Weekly*'s children's bestseller lists.

URL:
<http://www.bookwire.com>

The Good Girl's Soliloquy. Published by
Samuel Wood & Sons, New York, 1820.

Special Children's Literature Collections at Libraries

Chapter 6

Now that many scholars and researchers have access to the Internet and
sophisticated interlibrary loan systems, some people feel that it is no longer
necessary to visit special library collections in order to conduct research in
the field of children's literature. In my opinion, however, special children's
literature collections still serve as invaluable resources for certain types of
research. For scholars who are interested in conducting primary research on
the history of children's literature, such collections are indispensable. In
most cases, rare copies of historical children's books are not available
through interlibrary loan systems nor can they be accessed through the Internet. Scholars who are interested in examining the original manuscript versions of children's books are faced with a similar situation. Several special
collections have such manuscripts, but scholars must visit these collections in
order to see the manuscripts. In some cases, scholars want to conduct a survey of hundreds of children's books that deal with a certain subject. These
books may technically be available through interlibrary loan services, but it's
often easier to visit one special collection that already has these books
together than it is to fill out hundreds interlibrary loan request forms and
then wait for the books to come in over a period of several weeks.

People who are not engaged in formal research projects related to children's literature will still enjoy visiting some of these special children's literature collections. The collections often feature displays of rare children's
books and original manuscripts, and some of them sponsor special events
that are open to the public.

There are a great number of special children's literature collections
that are open to researchers. Dolores Blythe Jones identified over three hundred such collections in her book *Special Collections in Children's Literature: An
International Directory,* which was published by the American Library Association in 1995. The majority of these collections, however, are modest in size or
have a fairly narrow focus. Some are limited to children's authors from a particular state or region. Others are limited by subject matter. There are several
collections, for example, that consist of various nursery rhyme books. Since

Jones has already described the holdings of these smaller collections, I have not included them among the collections listed in this chapter. Instead, I have chosen to highlight twenty special collections that have extensive holdings related to children's literature.

AMERICAN JUVENILE LITERATURE COLLECTION OF THE AMERICAN ANTIQUARIAN SOCIETY As part of its mission to collect and preserve the early printed record of the United States, the American Antiquarian Society has long collected early American children's books and magazines. Its American Juvenile Literature Collection now consists of 17,000 children's books printed between 1700 and 1899. Some of the special strengths of this collection are its extensive holdings related to Jacob Abbott, Samuel Goodrich (aka Peter Parley), William Taylor Adams, and the McLoughlin Brothers publishing firm. It also has extensive periodical holdings, including *The Children's Magazine*, which is the first American children's periodical.

For more information:
Laura Wasowicz
Senior Cataloger
American Children's Books
   Project
American Antiquarian Society
185 Salisbury St.
Worcester, MA 01609
(508) 755-5221

THE BALDWIN LIBRARY OF HISTORICAL CHILDREN'S BOOKS For 30 years, Dr. Ruth Baldwin devoted much of her life to collecting historical children's books. She eventually donated her collection to the George A. Smathers Libraries at the University of Florida. Today the Baldwin Library of Historical Children's Literature contains approximately 90,000 volumes published in Great Britain and America from 1775 to 1950. The collection includes picture books, moral tales, adolescent fiction, adventure stories, poetry books, pop-ups, natural histories, geographies, biographies, and religious tracts. One of its unique strengths is its collection of 800 titles published in North America before 1820.

For more information:
Baldwin Library of Historical
   Children's Literature
Depart. of Special Collections
George A. Smathers Libraries
P.O. Box 117007
University of Florida
Gainesville, FL 32611
(352) 392-4788
email address: <ritsmit@
   nervm.nerdc.ufl.edu>

BUTLER LIBRARY Located at Columbia University, the Butler Library houses several special collections related to children's literature. The largest of these is its Historical Collection of Children's Literature, which consists of approximately 10,000 books and 450 periodicals. The Butler Library also has special collections related to Arthur Rackham, L. Frank Baum, Walter Farley, ABC books, and books bearing the imprint of the McLoughlin Brothers publishing firm.

For more information:
Butler Library
Rare Book and Manuscript
   Library
Columbia University
535 W. 114th St., Sixth Fl.
New York, NY 10027
(212) 854-2231

CENTER FOR THE STUDY OF BOOKS IN SPANISH FOR CHILDREN AND ADOLESCENTS Founded by Dr. Isabel Schon in 1989, the Center for the Study of Books in Spanish for Children and Adolescents endeavors to collect all the books in Spanish for children and adolescents published worldwide since 1989. The Center's holdings also include many children's books in Spanish published before 1989. Today the Center has over 50,000 books, but the collection is growing quickly. Schon anticipates that the Center will have over 100,000 books by the turn of the century.

For more information:
Center for the Study of Books
   in Spanish for Children
   and Adolescents
California State University,
   San Marcos
San Marcos, CA 92096-0001
(619) 750-4070
email: <ischon@mailhost1.
   csusm.edu>
Website: <http://www.csusm.
edu/campus_centers/csb>

THE CHILDREN'S LITERATURE CENTER OF THE LIBRARY OF CONGRESS Founded in 1963 as an information center within the Library of Congress, the Children's Literature Center provides researchers with access to approximately 180,000 children's books and related items. These books are scattered throughout the

For more information:
Library of Congress
Children's Literature Center
101 Independence Ave., S.E.
Washington, DC 20540-4620
(202) 707-5535

Library of Congress, but the Center's staff can provide users with assistance in retrieving whatever items they wish to examine. The Center also organizes lectures and publishes informative works about children's literature.

COOPERATIVE CHILDREN'S BOOK CENTER Established in 1963, the Cooperative Children's Book Center (CCBC) has a collection of approximately 35,000 children's books, including historical as well as contemporary works. Some of the special strengths of CCBC are its collection of alternative press books for children, its collection of materials by and about children's authors from Wisconsin, and its holdings related to multiculturalism.

For more information:
CCBC
4290 Helen C. White Hall
600 N. Park Street
Univ. of Wisconsin-Madison
Madison, WI 53706
(608) 263-3720
Website: <http://soemadison.
    wisc.edu/ccbc/>

COSTEN CHILDREN'S LIBRARY Located at Princeton University, the Costen Children's Library has one of the few special children's literature collections that is open to children. The collection consists of over 21,000 volumes as well as a number of manuscripts and original works of art. One of the major strengths of the collection is its holdings related to the famous children's book publisher John Newbery.

For more information:
Costen's Children's Library
Harvey S. Firestone Memorial
    Library
Princeton University
One Washington Road
Princeton, NJ 08544
(609) 258-3184

THE DE GRUMMOND CHILDREN'S LITERATURE COLLECTION Founded by Dr. Lena de Grummond, the de Grummond Children's Literature Collection consists of over 40,000 published books. It also has original manuscripts or illustrations from over 1,200 children's authors and illustrators. Dozens of children's magazines, dating from 1788 to the present, are also housed in the collection. Some of the special strengths of the collection are its extensive holdings related to Aesops fables, Kate Greenaway, Ezra Jack Keats, H.A. and Margaret Rey, and George Alfred Henty.

For more information:
Dolores Blythe Jones, Curator
de Grummond Children's
    Literature Collection
McCain Library and Archives
Box 5148
Univ. of Southern Mississippi
Hattiesburg, MS 39406-5148
(601) 266-4349
email: <dee.jones@usm.edu>
Website: <http://www.lib.usm.
    edu/degrumm.htm>

DETROIT PUBLIC LIBRARY The Rare Book Collection of the Detroit Public Library includes a wide variety of historical children's books and related items. Some of the special strengths of the collection are its extensive holdings related to Lewis Carroll, Kate Greenaway, Walter Crane, Wanda Ga'g, and Daniel Defoe.

For more information:
Rare Book Collection
Detroit Public Library
5201 Woodward Ave.
Detroit, MI 48202
(313) 833-1492

FALES LIBRARY Located at New York University, Fales Library has two large specialized collections that relate to children's literature. Its Alfred C. Berol Collection of Lewis Carroll is one of the world's largest collections of material about the life and writings of Lewis Carroll. Its Levy Dime Novel Collection is also one of the biggest collections of its kind. The Levy Collection contains more than 15,000 printed items, including story papers, periodicals, clothbound novels, and a large number of paperback series of American popular fiction.

For more information:
Fales Library
New York University
70 Washington Square South
New York, NY 10012-1091
(212) 998-2596

THE FREE LIBRARY OF PHILADELPHIA The Rare Book Department of the Free Library of Philadelphia houses approximately 60,000 items related to children's literature. These items are organized into ten different collections, each with its own emphasis. Its Early American Children's Books Collection contains

For more information:
DianeJude L. McDowell, Head
Children's Special Collections
Free Library of Philadelphia
1901 Vine St.
Philadelphia, PA 19103-1189

a wide variety of books ranging in date from 1682 to 1836. Its American Sunday-School Union Collection consists of 20,000 volumes that were published by this religious organization during the nineteenth century. Another of its collections focuses on European children's books. Also housed in the Free Library are collections that relate to Beatrix Potter, Kate Greenaway, Arthur Rackham, Robert Lawson, Munro Leaf, Howard Pyle, and A.B. Frost.

(215) 686-5370
Website: <http://www.library. phila.gov/central/ccd/ csc/ccsc.htm>

HUGHES CHILDREN'S LIBRARY   Part of the Chicago Public Library System, the Thomas Hughes Children's Library holds over 50,000 volumes, most of which date from 1900 to 1970. Some of the special strengths of the collection are its extensive holdings related to Mother Goose, folk and fairy tales, and Walt Disney.

For more information:
Thomas Hughes Children's
  Library
Harold Washington Library
400 S. State St.
Chicago, IL 60605
(312) 747-4200

THE JORDAN COLLECTION OF THE BOSTON PUBLIC LIBRARY   The Jordan Collection is a children's literature research collection containing over 157,000 volumes. Founded in 1967, the Collection is named in honor of Alice M. Jordan, the founder of children's services at the Boston Public Library. One of the special strengths of the Jordan Collection is its collection of children's books from foreign countries. Among its holdings are books from over one hundred different countries.

For more information:
Research Library Office
Boston Public Library
Copley Square
Boston, MA 02117
(617) 536-5400, ext. 239

KERLAN COLLECTION   Located at the University of Minnesota, the Kerlan Collection contains original materials, including manuscripts, artwork, galleys, and color proofs, for over 7,000 children's books. The collection also includes over 60,000 volumes, many of which are related to the original materials in the collection. Although its holdings include many historical books, the Kerlan Collection focuses primarily on contemporary American children's literature. Also located at the University of Minnesota are specialized collections of dime novels and series books for boys.

For more information:
Dr. Karen Hoyle, Curator
Kerlan Collection
109 Walter Library
117 Pleasant St. SE
University of Minnesota
Minneapolis, MN 55455
(612) 624-4576

LILLY LIBRARY   The Lilly Library, located at Indiana University, includes approximately 15,000 volumes and other items related to children's literature. For the most part, these volumes are part of the Elizabeth Ball Collection of Historical Children's Materials. The Lilly Library also has a special collection focusing on the works of George Cruikshank.

For more information:
The Lilly Library
Indiana University
Bloomington, IN 47405
(812) 855-2452

MORGAN LIBRARY'S EARLY CHILDREN'S BOOKS COLLECTION   The Pierpont Morgan Library in New York City houses a collection of approximately 10,000 early children's books and related materials. These books date from the third century A.D. to the early twentieth century. Among the special strengths of the collection are its holdings related to Lewis Carroll, Beatrix Potter, and Randolph Caldecott. It also has a sizable collection of French children's books.

For more information:
Anna Lou Ashby
Andrew W. Mellon Curator of
  Printed Books
The Pierpont Morgan Library
28 East 36th St.
New York, NY 10016-3490
(212) 685-0008
email: <bm.pmv@rlg.org>

THE NORTHEAST CHILDREN'S LITERATURE COLLECTION   Housed in the Thomas J. Dodd Research Center at the University of Connecticut, the Northeast Children's Literature Collection has a large collection of historical children's books. It also has manuscripts or original artwork from a number of children's

For more information:
Archives & Special Collections
Thomas J. Dodd Research Cntr.
405 Babbidge Rd., U-205
University of Connecticut
Storrs, CT 06269-1205

authors and illustrators, including Natalie Babbitt, Barbara Cooney, Eleanor Estes, Leonard Everett Fisher, Lillian Hoban, Nonny Hogrogian, Ruth Krauss, James Marshall, Barry Moser, Richard Scarry, and Esphyr Slobodkina.

(860) 486-4500
Website: <http://www.lib.uconn.edu/DoddCenter/ASC/asc.html>

POPULAR CULTURE LIBRARY   The Popular Culture Library was founded by Dr. Ray Browne in 1969 to support Bowling Green State University's various cultural studies programs. Many of the materials in the Popular Culture Library relate to children's literature, including series books, dime novels, Disney memorabilia, comic books, and Big Little Books.

For more information:
Popular Culture Library
Bowling Green State Univ.
Bowling Green, OH 43403-0600
(419) 372-2450

TORONTO PUBLIC LIBRARY   The Toronto Public Library has three important collections that relate to children's literature. Its Osborne Collection of Early Children's Books encompasses a wide variety of children's books ranging in date from the fourteenth century to 1910. Its Lillian H. Smith Collection focuses on children's books published in English since 1910. Its Canadiana Collection consists of a large selection of children's books in English related to Canada or whose writers, illustrators, or publishers are associated with Canada.

For more information:
Toronto Public Library
239 College Street
Toronto, Ontario
Canada M5T 1R5
(416) 393-7753

UCLA'S CHILDREN'S BOOK COLLECTION   Housed in the Research Library of the University of California at Los Angeles, the UCLA Children's Book Collection includes a wide variety of children's books and related items. Among the strengths of the collection are its holdings related to Maria Edgeworth, Marie Catherine d'Aulnoy, Edmund Evans, and Dr. Seuss.

For more information:
Special Collections
UCLA Research Library
405 Hilgard Ave.
Los Angeles, CA 90024
(310) 825-4879

Major Awards in Children's Literature

Chapter 7

In 1922, the American Library Association began awarding the Newbery Medal to an outstanding children's book, and ever since the granting of awards has played a major role in the history of children's literature. The Newbery Medal met with such success that the American Library Association decided to sponsor another award that would recognize outstanding picture books. Called the Caldecott Medal in honor of the famous illustrator Randolph Caldecott, this second award got its start in 1938. With the establishment of these awards, the American Library Association elevated the status of children's literature by drawing widespread attention each year to outstanding children's books. The publicity surrounding the granting of these awards also had the effect of propelling the creators of the winning books into the ranks of America's leading literary figures.

The creation of these awards also had a major impact on the publishing industry. Soon after these awards made their debuts, the publishers of the award-winning books noticed a sharp increase in sales. There were several reasons for these good sales figures. Most booksellers made sure they had these books in stock, librarians often ordered multiple copies for their shelves, and many teachers began using them in their classrooms. The publishers responded to these developments by ordering additional print runs and keeping the books in print for many years.

The Newbery and Caldecott Medals have received so much attention and support that other groups have begun granting awards to children's books. In most cases, these newer awards have focused on particular kinds of children's literature. While none of these awards has yet achieved the prestige associated with the Newbery and Caldecott Medals, some of them have succeeded in drawing attention to children's books that might otherwise have gone unnoticed by many readers. Among the most successful of the newer awards are the two Coretta Scott King Awards. Since 1970 a Coretta Scott King Award has been presented annually to an outstanding African American children's author, and since 1974 a second Coretta Scott King Award has been presented annually to an exceptional African American illustrator.

Perhaps because the winners of these various awards receive so much acclaim, it is easy to forget that an element of subjectivity always enters into the process of selecting the winning books. The granters of the Newbery Medal may say, for example, that it is given to the author of the "most distinguished contribution to children's literature" published during the preceding year, but it is actually impossible to proclaim with certainty which of all the thousands of children's books published in a year is the "most distinguished." Try as they might, the selectors of these awards cannot help but be influenced by their personal tastes in literature or the values and prejudices that are part of their cultural milieu. For such reasons, the selectors of these awards occasionally pass over wonderful children's books. Examples of classic children's books that did not win the Newbery Medal include Laura Ingalls Wilder's *Little House on the Prairie*, E. B. White's *Charlotte's Web* and Louise Fitzhugh's *Harriet the Spy*.

Recognizing that not all highly meritorious children's books win awards when they are first published, the Children's Literature Association established the Phoenix Award in order to honor children's books that have, over time, proven themselves worthy of special recognition. Since 1985, the Phoenix Award has been given to the author of a book that was published twenty years earlier and that did not receive a major award at the time of its original publication.

The winners of the Newbery Medal, the Caldecott Medal, the Coretta Scott King Awards, and the Phoenix Award are listed below. Information about some other children's book awards can be found at the end of this chapter. A complete and up-to-date list of children's book awards and their winners is provided in the 1996 edition of *Children's Books: Awards and Prizes*, published by the Children's Book Council.

Internet users can find listings of the winners of almost every children's book award in the English-speaking world at the following website: <http:/ /www.ucalgary.ca/~dkbrown/ awards.html>.

Newbery Medal

The Newbery Medal is named after John Newbery, an eighteenth-century British publisher of children's books. This award is now sponsored by the Association for Library Service to Children, which is a division of the American Library Association. The Newbery Medal is given to the author of the "most distinguished contribution" to children's literature published during the preceding year. Eligibility for this award is limited to citizens and permanent residents of the United States. In addition to naming the winning book, the selectors often designate one or more titles as Newbery Honor Books. More information about this award can be found in *The Newbery and Caldecott Awards: A Guide to the Medal and Honor Books, 1997 Edition*, published by the American Library Association. Both the winners and the honor books are listed below.

1922   *The Story of Mankind* by Hendrik Willem.

   Honor Books:

   The Great Quest by Charles Boardman Hawes.

   Cedric the Forester by Bernard G. Marshall.

   The Old Tobacco Shop by William Bowen.

   The Golden Fleece and the Heroes Who Lived Before Achilles by Padraic Colum.

   Windy Hill by Cornelia Meigs.

1923 *The Voyages of Doctor Dolittle* by Hugh Lofting.

1924 *The Dark Frigate* by Charles Boardman Hawes.

1925 *Tales from Silver Lands* by Charles J. Finger.
Honor Books:
Nicholas by Anne Carroll Moore.
Dream Coach by Anne and Dillwyn Parrish.

1926 *Shen of the Sea* by Arthur Bowie Chrisman.
Honor Book:
The Voyagers by Padraic Colum.

1927 *Smokey, the Cowhorse* by Will James.

1928 *Gay-Neck, The Story of a Pigeon* by Dhan Gopal Mukerji.
Honor Books:
The Wonder Smith and His Sons by Ella Young.
Downright Dencey by Caroline Dale Snedeker.

1929 *The Trumpeter of Krakow* by Eric P. Kelly.
Honor Books:
The Pigtail of Ah Lee Ben Loo by John Bennett.
Millions of Cats by Wanda Ga'g.
The Boy Who Was by Grace T. Hallock.
Clearing Weather by Cornelia Meigs.
The Runaway Papoose by Grace P. Moon.
Tod of the Fens by Eleanor Whitney.

1930 *Hitty: Her First Hundred Years* by Rachel Field.
Honor Books:
The Tangle-Coated Horse and Other Tales: Episodes from the Fionn Saga by Ella Young.
Vaino: A Boy of New Finland by Julia Davis Adams.
Pran of Albania by Elizabeth C. Miller.
The Jumping-Off Place by Marian Hurd McNeely.
A Daughter of the Seine by Jeanette Eaton.
Little Blacknose by Hildegarde Hoyt Swift.

1931 *The Cat Who Went to Heaven* by Elizabeth Coatsworth.
Honor Books:
Floating Island by Anne Parrish.
The Dark Star of Itza by Alida Malkus.
Queer Person by Ralph Hubbard.
Mountains Are Free by Julia Davis Adams.
Spice and the Devil's Cave by Agnes D. Hewes.
Meggy McIntosh by Elizabeth Janet Gray.
Garram the Hunter: A Boy of the Hill Tribes by Herbert Best.
Ood-Le-Uk, The Wanderer by Alice Lide and Margaret Johansen.

1932   *Waterless Mountain* by Laura Adams Armer.
        Honor Books:
        The Fairy Circus by Dorothy Lathrop.
        Calico Bush by Rachel Field.
        Boy of the South Seas by Eunice Tietjens.
        Out of the Flame by Eloise Lownsbery.
        Jane's Island by Marjorie Hill Alee.
        The Truce of the Wolf and Other Tales of Old Italy by Mary Gould Davis.

1933   *Young Fu of the Upper Yangtze* by Elizabeth Foreman.
        Honor Books:
        Swift Rivers by Cornelia Meigs.
        The Railroad to Freedom by Hildegarde Swift.
        Children of the Soil by Nora Burglon.

1934   *Invincible Louisa: The Story of the Author of "Little Women"* by Cornelia Meigs.
        Honor Books:
        The Forgotten Daughter by Caroline Dale Snedeker.
        Swords of Steel by Elsie Singmaster.
        ABC Bunny by Wanda Ga'g.
        Winged Girl of Knossos by Erick Berry.
        New Land by Sarah L. Schmidt.
        The Apprentice of Florence by Anne Kyle.
        The Big Tree of Bunlahy: Stories of My Own Countryside by Padraic Colum.
        Glory of the Seas by Agnes D. Hewes.

1935   *Dobry* by Monica Shannon.
        Honor Books:
        The Pageant of Chinese History by Elizabeth Seeger.
        Davy Crockett by Constance Rourke.
        A Day on Skates: The Story of a Dutch Picnic by Hilda Van Stockum.

1936   *Caddie Woodlawn* by Carol Ryrie Brink.
        Honor Books:
        Honk: The Moose by Phil Strong.
        The Good Master by Kate Seredy.
        Young Walter Scott by Elizabeth Janet Gray.
        All Sail Set by Armstrong Sperry.

1937   *Roller Skates* by Ruth Sawyer.
        Honor Books:
        Phoebe Fairchild: Her Book by Lois Lenski.
        Whistler's Van by Idwal Jones.
        The Golden Basket by Ludwig Bemelmans.
        Winterbound by Margery Bianco.

Audubon by Constance Rourke.

The Codfish Musket by Agnes D. Hewes.

1938   *The White Stag* by Kate Seredy.

Honor Books:

Bright Island by Mabel L. Robinson.

Pecos Bill by James Cloyd Bowman.

On the Banks of Plum Creek by Laura Ingalls Wilder.

1939   *Thimble Summer* by Elizabeth Enright.

Honor Books:

Leader by Destiny: George Washington, Man and Patriot by Jeanette Eaton.

Penn by Elizabeth Janet Gray.

Nino by Valenti Angelo.

"Hello, the Boat!" by Phyllis Crawford.

Mr. Popper's Penguins by Richard and Florence Atwater.

1940   *Daniel Boone* by James H. Daugherty.

Honor Books:

The Singing Tree by Kate Seredy.

Runner of the Mountain Tops by Mabel L. Robinson.

By the Shores of Silver Lake by Laura Ingalls Wilder.

Boy with a Pack by Stephen W. Meader.

1941   *Call It Courage* by Armstrong Sperry.

Honor Books:

Blue Willow by Doris Gates.

Young Mac of Fort Vancouver by Mary Jane Carr.

The Long Winter by Laura Ingalls Wilder.

Nansen by Anna Gertrude Hall.

1942   *The Matchlock Gun* by Walter D. Edmunds.

Honor Books:

Little Town on the Prairie by Laura Ingalls Wilder.

George Washington's World by Genevieve Foster.

Indian Captive: The Story of Mary Jemison by Lois Lenski.

Down Ryton Water by Eva Roe Gaggin.

1943   *Adam of the Road* by Elizabeth Janet Gray.

Honor Books:

The Middle Moffat by Eleanor Estes.

"Have You Seen Tom Thumb?" by Mabel Leigh Hunt.

1944   *Johnny Tremain* by Esther Forbes.

Honor Books:

These Happy Golden Years by Laura Ingalls Wilder.

Fog Magic by Julia L. Sauer.

Rufus M. by Eleanor Estes.

Mountain Born by Elizabeth Yates.

1945   *Rabbit Hill* by Robert Lawson.
          Honor Books:
          The Hundred Dresses by Eleanor Estes.
          The Silver Pencil by Alice Dalgliesh.
          Abraham Lincoln's World by Genevieve Foster.
          Lone Journey: The Life of Roger Williams by Jeanette Eaton.

1946   *Strawberry Hill* by Lois Lenski.
          Honor Books:
          Justin Morgan Had a Horse by Marguerite Henry.
          The Moved-Outers by Florence Crannell Means.
          Bhimsa, the Dancing Bear by Christine Weston.
          New Found World by Katherine B. Shippen.

1947   *Miss Hickory* by Carolyn Sherwin Bailey.
          Honor Books:
          The Wonderful Year by Nancy Barnes.
          The Big Tree by Mary and Conrad Buff.
          The Heavenly Tenants by William Maxwell.
          The Avion My Uncle Flew by Cyrus Fisher.
          The Hidden Treasure of Glaston by Eleanore M. Jewett.

1948   *The Twenty-One Balloons* by William Pène du Bois.
          Honor Books:
          Pancakes-Paris by Claire Huchet Bishop.
          Li Lun, Lad of Courage by Carolyn Treffinger.
          The Quaint and Curious Quest of Johnny Longfoot, The Shoe-King's Son by Catherine Besterman.
          The Cow-Tail Switch, And Other West African Stories by Harold Courlander and George Herzog.
          Misty of Chincoteague by Marguerite Henry.

1949   *King of the Wind* by Marguerite Henry.
          Honor Books:
          Seabird by Holling Clancy Holling.
          Daughter of the Mountains by Louise Rankin.
          My Father's Dragon by Ruth S. Gannett.
          Story of the Negro by Arna Bontemps.

1950   *The Door in the Wall* by Marguerite de Angeli.
          Honor Books:
          Tree of Freedom by Rebecca Caudill.
          The Blue Cat of Castle Town by Catherine Coblentz.
          Kildee House by Rutherford Montgomery.
          George Washington by Genevieve Foster.
          Song of the Pines by Walter and Marion Havighurst.

1951   *Amos Fortune, Free Man* by Elizabeth Yates.
          Honor Books:
          Better Known as Johnny Appleseed by Mabel Leigh.

Gandhi, Fighter Without a Sword by Jeanette Eaton.

Abraham Lincoln, Friend of the People by Clara I. Judson.

The Story of Appleby Capple by Anne Parrish.

1952   *Ginger Pye* by Eleanor Estes.

Honor Books:

Americans Before Columbus by Elizabeth Chesley Baity.

Minn of the Mississippi by Holling Clancy Holling.

The Defender by Nicholas Kalashnikoff.

The Light at Tern Rock by Julia L. Sauer.

The Apple and the Arrow by Mary and Conrad Buff.

1953   *Secret of the Andes* by Ann Nolan Clark.

Honor Books:

Charlotte's Web by E. B. White.

Moccasin Trail by Eloise J. McGraw.

Red Sails to Capri by Ann Weil.

The Bears on Hemlock Mountain by Alice Dalgliesh.

Birthdays of Freedom, Vol. 1 by Genevieve Foster.

1954   *And Now Miguel* by Joseph Krumgold.

Honor Books:

All Alone by Claire Huchet Bishop.

Shadrach by Meindert DeJong.

Hurry Home, Candy by Meindert DeJong.

Theodore Roosevelt, Fighting Patriot by Clara I. Judson.

Magic Maize by Mary and Conrad Buff.

1955   *The Wheel on the School* by Meindert DeJong.

Honor Books:

The Courage of Sarah Noble by Alice Dalgliesh.

Banner in the Sky by James Ramsey Ullman.

1956   *Carry on, Mr. Bowditch* by Jean Lee Latham.

Honor Books:

The Golden Name Day by Jennie D. Lindquist.

The Secret River by Marjorie Kinnan Rawlings.

Men, Microscopes and Living Things by Katherine B. Shippen.

1957   *Miracles on Maple Hill* by Virginia Sorensen.

Honor Books:

Old Yeller by Fred Gipson.

The House of Sixty Fathers by Meindert DeJong.

Mr. Justice Holmes by Clara I. Judson.

The Corn Grows Ripe by Dorothy Rhoads.

The Black Fox of Lorne by Marguerite de Angeli.

1958   *Rifles for Watie* by Harold Keith.

Honor Books:
The Horsecatcher by Mari Sandoz.
Gone-Away Lake by Elizabeth Enright.
The Great Wheel by Robert Lawson.
Tom Paine, Freedom's Apostle by Leo Gurko.

1959   *The Witch of Blackbird Pond* by Elizabeth George Speare.
Honor Books:
The Family Under the Bridge by Natalie S. Carlson.
Along Came a Dog by Meindert DeJong.
Chucaro: Wild Pony of the Pampa by Francis Kalnay.
The Perilous Road by William O. Steele.

1960   *Onion John* by Joseph Krumgold.
Honor Books:
My Side of the Mountain by Jean George.
America Is Born by Gerald Johnson.
The Gammage Cup by Carol Kendall.

1961   *Island of the Blue Dolphins* by Scott O'Dell.
Honor Books:
America Moves Forward by Gerald Johnson.
Old Ramon by Jack Schaefer.
The Cricket in Times Square by George Selden.

1962   *The Bronze Bow* by Elizabeth George Speare.
Honor Books:
Frontier Living by Edwin Tunis.
The Golden Goblet by Eloise J. McGraw.
Belling the Tiger by Mary Stolz.

1963   *A Wrinkle in Time* by Madeleine L'Engle.
Honor Books:
Thistle and Thyme by Sorche Nic Leodhas.
Men of Athens by Olivia Coolidge.

1964   *It's Like This, Cat* by Emily Cheney Neville.
Honor Books:
Rascal by Sterling North.
The Loner by Esther Wier.

1965   *Shadow of a Bull* by Maia Wojciechowska.
Honor Book:
Across Five Aprils by Irene Hunt.

1966   *I, Juan de Pareja* by Elizabeth Borton de Treviño.
Honor Books:
The Black Cauldron by Lloyd Alexander.
The Animal Family by Randall Jarrell.
The Noonday Friends by Mary Stolz.

1967 *Up the Road Slowly* by Irene Hunt.
Honor Books:
The King's Fifth by Scott O'Dell.
Zlateh the Goat and Other Stories by Isaac Bashevis Singer.
The Jazz Man by Mary H. Weik.

1968 *From the Mixed-Up Files of Mrs. Basil E. Frankweiler*
by E.L. Konigsburg.
Honor Books:
Jennifer, Hecate, Macbeth, William McKinley, and Me, Elizabeth by
E. L. Konigsburg.
The Black Pearl by Scott O'Dell.
The Fearsome Inn by Isaac Bashevis Singer.
The Egypt Game by Zilpha Keatley Snyder.

1969 *The High King* by Lloyd Alexander.
Honor Books:
To Be a Slave by Julius Lester.
When Shlemiel Went to Warsaw and Other Stories by Isaac Bashevis
Singer.

1970 *Sounder* by William H. Armstrong.
Honor Books:
Our Eddie by Sulamith Ish-Kishor.
The Many Ways of Seeing: An Introduction to the Pleasures of Art
by Janet Gaylord Moore.
Journey Outside by Mary Q. Steele.

1971 *Summer of Swans* by Betsy Byars.
Honor Books:
Kneeknock Rise by Natalie Babbitt.
Enchantress from the Stars by Sylvia Louise Engdahl.
Sing Down the Moon by Scott O'Dell.

1972 *Mrs. Frisby and the Rats of NIMH* by Robert O'Brien.
Honor Books:
Incident at Hawk's Hill by Allen W. Eckert.
The Planet of Junior Brown by Virginia Hamilton.
The Tombs of Atuan by Ursula K. LeGuin.
Annie and the Old One by Miska Miles.
The Headless Cupid by Zilpha Keatley Snyder.

1973 *Julie of the Wolves* by Jean Craighead George.
Honor Books:
Frog and Toad Together by Arnold Lobel.
The Upstairs Room by Johanna Reiss.
The Witches of Worm by Zilpha Keatley Snyder.

1974 *The Slave Dancer* by Paula Fox.
Honor Book:
The Dark Is Rising by Susan Cooper.

1975 *M. C. Higgins the Great* by Virginia Hamilton.
Honor Books:
Figgs & Phantoms by Ellen Raskin.
My Brother Sam Is Dead by James Lincoln Collier and Christopher Collier.
The Perilous Gard by Elizabeth Marie Pope.
Philip Hall Likes Me, I Reckon Maybe by Bette Greene.

1976 *The Grey King* by Susan Cooper.
Honor Books:
The Hundred Penny Box by Sharon Bell Mathis.
Dragonwings by Laurence Yep.

1977 *Roll of Thunder, Hear My Cry* by Mildred D. Taylor.
Honor Books:
Abel's Island by William Steig.
A String in the Harp by Nancy Bond.

1978 *Bridge to Terabithia* by Katherine Paterson.
Honor Books:
Anpao: An American Indian Odyssey by Jamake Highwater.
Ramona and Her Father by Beverly Cleary.

1979 *The Westing Game* by Ellen Raskin.
Honor Book:
The Great Gilly Hopkins by Katherine Paterson.

1980 *A Gathering of Days: A New England Girl's Journal, 1930–32* by Joan Blos.
Honor Book:
The Road from Home: The Story of an Armenian Girl by David Kherdian.

1981 *Jacob Have I Loved* by Katherine Paterson.
Honor Books:
The Fledgling by Jane Langton.
A Ring of Endless Light by Madeleine L'Engle.

1982 *A Visit to William Blake's Inn: Poems for Innocent and Experienced Travelers* by Nancy Willard.
Honor Books:
Ramona Quimby, Age 8 by Beverly Cleary.
Upon the Head of a Goat: A Childhood in Hungary, 1939-1944 by Aranka Siegal.

1983 *Dicey's Song* by Cynthia Voight.
Honor Books:
The Blue Sword by Robin McKinley.
Dr. DeSoto by William Steig.
Graven Images by Paul Fleischman.
Homesick: My Own Story by Jean Fritz.
Sweet Whispers, Brother Rush by Virginia Hamilton.

1984 *Dear Mr. Henshaw* by Beverly Cleary.
Honor Books:
The Sign of the Beaver by Elizabeth George Speare.
A Solitary Blue by Cynthia Voight.
Sugaring Time by Kathryn Lasky.
The Wish Giver by Bill Brittain.

1985 *The Hero and the Crown* by Robin McKinley.
Honor Books:
Like Jake and Me by Mavis Jukes.
The Moves Make the Man by Bruce Brooks.
One-Eyed Cat by Paula Fox.

1986 *Sarah, Plain and Tall* by Patricia MacLachlan.
Honor Books:
Commodore Perry in the Land of Shogun by Rhonda Blumberg.
Dogsong by Gary Paulsen.

1987 *The Whipping Boy* by Sid Fleischman.
Honor Books:
On My Honor by Marion Dane Bauer.
Volcano: The Eruption of Healing of Mount St. Helens by Patricia Lauber.
A Fine White Dust by Cynthia Rylant.

1988 *Lincoln: A Photobiography* by Russell Freedman.
Honor Books:
After the Rain by Norma Fox Mazer.
Hatchet by Gary Paulsen.

1989 *Joyful Noise: Poems for Two Voices* by Paul Fleischman.
Honor Books:
In the Beginning: Creation Stories from Around the World by Virginia Hamilton.
Scorpions by Walter Dean Myers.

1990 *Number the Stars* by Lois Lowry.
Honor Books:
Afternoon of the Elves by Janet Taylor Lisle.
Shabanu, Daughter of the Wind by Suzanne Fisher Staples.
The Winter Room by Gary Paulsen.

1991 *Maniac Magee* by Jerry Spinelli.
Honor Book:
The True Confessions of Charlotte Doyle by Avi.

1992 *Shiloh* by Phyllis Reynolds Naylor.
Honor Books:
Nothing But the Truth by Avi.

The Wright Brothers: How They Invented the Airplane
by Russell Freedman.

1993   *Missing May* by Cynthia Rylant.

Honor Books:

The Dark-Thirty: Southern Tales of the Supernatural by Patricia McKissack.

Somewhere in Darkness by Walter Dean Myers.

What Hearts by Bruce Brooks.

1994   *The Giver* by Lois Lowry.

Honor Books:

Crazy Lady by Jane Leslie Conly.

Dragon's Gate by Laurence Yep.

Eleanor Roosevelt: A Life of Discovery by Russell Freedman.

1995   *Walk Two Moons* by Sharon Creech.

Honor Books:

Catherine, Called Birdy by Karen Cushman.

The Ear, the Eye and the Arm by Nancy Farmer.

1996   *The Midwife's Apprentice* by Karen Cushman.

Honor Books:

What Jamie Saw by Carolyn Coman.

The Watsons Go to Birmingham - 1963 by Christopher Paul Curtis.

Yolanda's Genius by Carol Fenner.

The Great Fire by Jim Murphy.

1997   *The View from Saturday* by E.L. Konigsburg.

Honor Books:

A Girl Named Disaster by Nancy Farmer.

Moorchild by Eloise McGraw.

The Thief by Megan Whalen Turner.

Belle Prater's Boy by Ruth White.

Caldecott Medal

The Caldecott Medal is named after Randolph Caldecott, a nineteenth-century British illustrator of children's books. This award is now sponsored by the Association for Library Service to Children, which is a division of the American Library Association. The Caldecott Medal is given to the illustrator of the "most distinguished picture book" published during the preceding year. Eligibility for this award is limited to citizens and permanent residents of the United States. In addition to naming the winning book, the selectors often designate one or more titles as Caldecott Honor Books. More information about this award can be found in *The Newbery and Caldecott Awards: A Guide to the Medal and Honor Books, 1997 Edition*, published by the American Library Association. Both the winners and the honor books are listed on the pages that follow.

1938 *Animals of the Bible, a Picture Book* edited by Helen Dean Fish. Illustrated by Dorothy P. Lathrop.
Honor Books:
Seven Simeons: A Russian Tale by Boris Artzybasheff.
Four and Twenty Blackbirds compiled by Helen Dean Fish. Illustrated by Robert Lawson.

1939 *Mei Li* by Thomas Handforth.
Honor Books:
The Forest Pool by Laura Adams Armer.
Wee Gillis by Munro Leaf. Illustrated by Robert Lawson.
Snow White and the Seven Dwarfs by Wanda Ga'g.
Barkis by Clare Newberry.
Andy and the Lion by James Daugherty

1940 *Abraham Lincoln* by Ingri d'Aulaire and Edgar Parin d'Aulaire.
Honor Books:
Cock-a-Doodle-Doo by Berta and Elmer Hader.
Madeline by Ludwig Bemelmans.
The Ageless Story by Lauren Ford.

1941 *They Were Strong and Good* by Robert Lawson.
Honor Book:
April's Kitten by Clare Turlay Newberry.

1942 *Make Way for Ducklings* by Robert McCloskey.
Honor Books:
An American ABC by Maud and Miska Petersham.
In My Mother's House by Ann Nolan Clark. Illustrated by Velino Herrera
Paddle-to-the-Sea by Holling Clancy Holling.
Nothing at All by Wanda Ga'g.

1943 *The Little House* by Virginia Lee Burton.
Honor Books:
Dash and Dart by Mary and Conrad Buff.
Marshmallow by Clare Turlay Newberry.

1944 *Many Moons* by James Thurber. Illustrated by Louis Slobodkin.
Honor Books:
Small Rain: Verses from the Bible edited by Jessie Orton Jones. Illustrated by Elizabeth Orton Jones.
Pierre Pigeon by Lee Kingman. Illustrated by Arnold Edwin Bare.
The Mighty Hunter by Berta and Elmer Hader.
A Child's Good Night Book by Margaret Wise Brown. Illustrated by Jean Charlot.
Good Luck Horse by Chih-Yi Chan. Illustrated by Plato Chan.

1945 *Prayer for a Child* by Rachel Field. Illustrated by Elizabeth Orton Jones.

Honor books:

Mother Goose: Seventy-Seven Verses With Pictures by Tasha Tudor.

In the Forest by Marie Hall Ets.

Yonie Wondernose by Marguerite de Angeli.

The Christmas Anna Angel by Ruth Sawyer. Illustrated by Kate Seredy.

1946   *The Rooster Crows* by Maud and Miska Petersham.

Honor Books:

Little Lost Lamb by Golden MacDonald. Illustrated by Leonard Weisgard.

Sing Mother Goose by Opal Wheeler. Illustrated by Marjorie Torrey.

My Mother Is the Most Beautiful Woman in the World by Becky Reyher. Illustrated by Ruth Gannett.

You Can Write Chinese by Kurt Wiese.

1947   *The Little Island* by Golden MacDonald. Illustrated by Leonard Weisgard.

Honor Books:

Rain Drop Splash by Alvin Tresselt. Illustrated by Leonard Weisgard.

Boats on the River by Marjorie Flack. Illustrated by Jay Hyde Barnum.

Timothy Turtle by Al Graham. Illustrated by Tony Palazzo.

Pedro, the Angel of Olvera Street by Leo Politi.

Sing in Praise: A Collection of the Best Loved Hymns by Opal Wheeler. Illustrated by Marjorie Torrey.

1948   *White Snow, Bright Snow* by Alvin Tresselt. Illustrated by Roger Duvoisin.

Honor Books:

Stone Soup: An Old Tale by Marcia Brown.

McElligot's Pool by Dr. Seuss.

Bambino the Clown by George Schreiber.

Roger and the Fox by Lavinia Davis. Illustrated by Hildegard Woodward.

Song of Robin Hood edited by Anne Malcolmson. Illustrated by Virginia Lee Burton.

1949   *The Big Snow* by Berta and Elmer Hader.

Honor Books:

Blueberries for Sal by Robert McCloskey

All Around Town by Phyllis McGinley. Illustrated by Helen Stone.

Juanita by Leo Politi.

Fish in the Air by Kurt Wiese.

1950   *Song of the Swallows* Leo Politi.

Honor Books:

America's Ethan Allen by Stewart Holbrook. Illustrated by Lynd Ward.

The Wild Birthday Cake by Lavinia R. Davis. Illustrated by Hildegard Woodward.

The Happy Day by Ruth Krauss. Illustrated by Marc Simont.

Henry-Fisherman by Marcia Brown.

Bartholomew and the Oobleck by Dr. Seuss.

1951 *The Egg Tree* by Katherine Milhous.

Honor Books:

Dick Whittington and His Cat by Marcia Brown.

The Two Reds by William Lipkind. Illustrated by Nicholas Mordvinoff.

If I Ran the Zoo by Dr. Seuss.

T-Bone, the Baby-Sitter by Clare Turlay Newberry.

The Most Wonderful Doll in the World by Phyllis McGinley. Illustrated by Helen Stone.

1952 *Finders Keepers* by William Lipkind. Illustrated by Nicholas Mordvinoff.

Honor Books:

Mr. T. W. Anthony Woo by Marie Hall Ets.

Skipper John's Cook by Marcia Brown

All Falling Down by Gene Zion. Illustrated by Margaret Bloy Graham.

Bear Party by William Pène du Bois.

Feather Mountain by Elizabeth Olds.

1953 *The Biggest Bear* by Lynd Ward.

Honor Books:

Puss in Boots by Marcia Brown.

One Morning in Maine by Robert McCloskey.

Ape in a Cape: An Alphabet of Odd Animals by Fritz Eichenberg.

The Storm Book by Charlotte Zolotow. Illustrated by Margaret Bloy Graham.

Five Little Monkeys by Juliet Kepes.

1954 *Madeline's Rescue* by Ludwig Bemelmans.

Honor Books:

Journey Cake, Ho! by Ruth Sawyer. Illustrated by Robert McCloskey.

When Will the World Be Mine? by Miriam Schlein. Illustrated by Jean Charlot.

The Steadfast Tin Soldier by Hans Christian Andersen. Translated by M. R. James. Illustrated by Marcia Brown.

A Very Special House by Ruth Krauss. Illustrated by Maurice Sendak.

Green Eyes by Abe Birnbaum.

1955 *Cinderella, or the Little Glass Slipper* by Charles Perrault. Translated and illustrated by Marcia Brown.

> **Honor Books:**
>
> *Book of Nursery and Mother Goose Rhymes* by Marguerite de Angeli.
>
> *Wheel on the Chimney* by Margaret Wise Brown. Illustrated by Tibor Gergely.
>
> *The Thanksgiving Story* by Alice Dalgliesh. Illustrated by Helen Sewell.

1956 *Frog Went A-Courtin'* by John Langstaff. Illustrated by Feodor Rojankovsky.

> **Honor Books:**
>
> *Play With Me* by Marie Hall Ets.
>
> *Crow Boy* by Taro Yashima.

1957 *A Tree Is Nice* by Janice May Udry. Illustrated by Marc Simont.

> **Honor Books:**
>
> *Mr. Penny's Race Horse* by Marie Hall Ets.
>
> *1 Is One* by Tasha Tudor.
>
> *Anatole* by Eve Titus. Illustrated by Paul Galdone.
>
> *Gillespie and the Guards* by Benjamin Elkin. Illustrated by James Daugherty.
>
> *Lion* by William Pène du Bois.

1958 *Time of Wonder* by Robert McCloskey.

> **Honor Books:**
>
> *Fly High, Fly Low* by Don Freeman.
>
> *Anatole and the Cat* by Eve Titus. Illustrated by Paul Galdone.

1959 *Chanticleer and the Fox* by Chaucer. Adapted and illustrated by Barbara Cooney.

> **Honor Books:**
>
> *The House That Jack Built ("La Maison Que Jacques a Bâtie"): A Picture Book in Two Languages* by Antonio Frasconi.
>
> *What Do You Say, Dear? A Book of Manners for All Occasions* by Sesyle Joslin. Illustrated by Maurice Sendak.
>
> *Umbrella* by Taro Yashima.

1960 *Nine Days to Christmas* by Marie Hall Ets and Aurora Labastida.

> **Honor Books:**
>
> *Houses by the Sea* by Alice E. Goudey. Illustrated by Adrienne Adams.
>
> *The Moon Jumpers* by Janice May Udry. Illustrated by Maurice Sendak.

1961 *Baboushka and the Three Kings* by Ruth Robbins. Illustrated by Nicolas Sidjakov.

> **Honor Book:**
>
> *Inch by Inch* by Leo Lionni.

1962 *Once a Mouse* by Marcia Brown.

Honor Books:

The Fox Went Out on a Chilly Night: An Old Song by Peter Spier.

Little Bear's Visit by Else Minarik. Illustrated by Maurice Sendak.

The Day We Saw the Sun Come Up by Alice Goudey. Illustrated by Adrienne Adams.

1963 *The Snowy Day* by Ezra Jack Keats

Honor Books:

The Sun Is a Golden Earring by Natalia Belting. Illustrated by Bernarda Bryson.

Mr. Rabbit and the Lovely Present by Charlotte Zolotow. Illustrated by Maurice Sendak.

1964 *Where the Wild Things Are* by Maurice Sendak.

Honor Books:

Swimmy by Leo Lionni.

All in the Morning Early by Sorche Nic Leodhas. Illustrated by Evaline Ness.

Mother Goose and Nursery Rhymes by Philip Reed.

1965 *May I Bring a Friend?* by Beatrice Schenk de Regniers. Illustrated by Beni Montresor.

Honor Books:

Rain Makes Applesauce by Julian Scheer. Illustrated by Marvin Bileck.

The Wave by Margaret Hodges. Illustrated by Blair Lent.

A Pocketful of Cricket by Rebecca Caudill. Illustrated by Evaline Ness.

1966 *Always Room for One More* by Sorche Nic Leodhas. Illustrated by Nonny Hogrogian.

Honor Books:

Hide and Seek Fog by Alvin Tresselt. Illustrated by Roger Duvoisin.

Just Me by Marie Hall Ets.

Tom Tit Tot adapted by Joseph Jacobs. Illustrated by Evaline Ness.

1967 *Sam, Bangs and Moonshine* by Evaline Ness.

Honor Book:

One Wide River to Cross adapted by Barbara Emberley. Illustrated by Ed Emberley.

1968 *Drummer Hoff* adapted by Barbara Emberley. Illustrated by Ed Emberley.

Honor Books:

Frederick by Leo Lionni.

Seashore Story by Taro Yashima.

The Emperor and the Kite by Jane Yolen. Illustrated by Ed Young.

1969 *The Fool of the World and the Flying Ship: A Russian Tale* by Arthur Ransome. Illustrated by Uri Shulevitz.

Honor Book:

Why the Sun and the Moon Live in the Sky: An African Folktale by Elphinstone Dayrell. Illustrated by Blair Lent.

1970 *Sylvester and the Magic Pebble* by William Steig.

Honor Books:

Goggles! by Ezra Jack Keats.

Alexander and the Wind-Up Mouse by Leo Lionni.

Pop Corn and Ma Goodness by Edna Mitchell Preston. Illustrated by Robert Andrew Parker.

Thy Friend, Obadiah by Brinton Turkle.

The Judge: An Untrue Tale by Harve Zemach. Illustrated by Margot Zemach.

1971 *A Story, a Story: An African Tale* by Gail E. Haley

Honor Books:

The Angry Moon by William Sleator. Illustrated by Blair Lent.

Frog and Toad Are Friends by Arnold Lobel.

In the Night Kitchen by Maurice Sendak.

1972 *One Fine Day* by Nonny Hogrogian

If All the Seas Were One Sea by Janina Domanska.

Moja Means One: Swahili Counting Book by Muriel Feelings. Illustrated by Tom Feelings.

Hildilid's Night by Cheli Duran Ryan. Illustrated by Arnold Lobel.

1973 *The Funny Little Woman* by Arlene Mosel. Illustrated by Blair Lent.

Honor Books:

Hosie's Alphabet by Hosea Baskin, Tobias Baskin, and Lisa Baskin. Illustrated by Leonard Baskin.

When Clay Sings by Byrd Baylor. Illustrated by Tom Bahti.

Snow-White and the Seven Dwarfs by the Brothers Grimm. Illustrated by Nancy Ekholm Burkert.

Anansi the Spider: A Tale from the Ashanti by Gerald McDermott.

1974 *Duffy and the Devil* by Harve Zemach. Illustrated by Margot Zemach.

Honor Books:

Three Jovial Huntsmen by Susan Jeffers.

Cathedral: The Story of Its Construction by David Macaulay.

1975 *Arrow to the Sun* by Gerald McDermott.

Honor Book:

Jambo Means Hello: Swahili Alphabet Book by Muriel Feelings. Illustrated by Tom Feelings.

1976 *Why Mosquitoes Buzz in People's Ears* by Verna Aardema. Illustrated by Leo and Diane Dillon.

Honor Books:

The Dessert Is Theirs by Byrd Baylor. Illustrated by Peter Parnall.

Strega Nona by Tomie dePaola.

1977 *Ashanti to Zulu: African Traditions* by Margaret Musgrove. Illustrated by Leo and Diane Dillon.

Honor Books:

The Amazing Bone by William Steig.

The Contest by Nonny Hogrogian.

Fish for Supper by M. B. Goffstein.

The Golem: A Jewish Legend by Beverly Brodsky McDermott.

Hawk, I'm Your Brother by Byrd Baylor. Illustrated by Peter Parnall.

1978 *Noah's Ark* by Peter Spier.

Honor Books:

Castle by David Macaulay.

It Could Always Be Worse by Margot Zemach.

1979 *The Girl Who Loved Wild Horses* by Paul Goble.

Honor Books:

Freight Train by Donald Crews.

The Way to Start a Day by Byrd Baylor. Illustrated by Peter Parnall.

1980 *Ox-Cart Man* by Donald Hall. Illustrated by Barbara Cooney.

Ben's Trumpet by Rachel Isadora.

The Treasure by Uri Schulevitz.

The Garden of Abdul Gasazi by Chris Van Allsburg.

1981 *Fables* by Arnold Lobel.

The Bremen-Town Musicians by Ilse Plume

The Grey Lady and the Strawberry Snatcher by Molly Bang.

Mice Twice by Joseph Low.

Truck by Donald Crews.

1982 *Jumanji* by Chris Van Allsburg.

Honor Books:

A Visit to William Blake's Inn: Poems for Innocent and Experienced Travelers by Nancy Willard. Illustrated by Alice and Martin Provensen.

Where the Buffaloes Begin by Olaf Baker. Illustrated by Stephen Gammell.

On Market Street by Arnold Lobel. Illustrated by Anita Lobel.

Outside Over There by Maurice Sendak.

1983 *Shadow* by Blaise Cendrars. Illustrated by Marcia Brown.

Honor Books:

When I Was Young in the Mountains by Cynthia Rylant. Illustrated by Diane Goode.

A Chair for My Mother by Vera B. Williams.

1984 *The Glorious Flight: Across the Channel with Louis Blériot* by Alice and Martin Provensen.

Honor Books:

Ten, Nine, Eight by Molly Bang.

Little Red Riding Hood by Trina Schart Hyman.

1985 *Saint George and the Dragon* by Margaret Hodges. Illustrated by Trina Schart Hyman.

Honor Books:

Hansel and Gretel by Rika Lesser. Illustrated by Paul O. Zelinsky.

The Story of Jumping Mouse by John Steptoe.

Have You Seen My Duckling? by Nancy Tafuri.

1986 *The Polar Express* by Chris Van Allsburg.

Honor Books:

The Relatives Came by Cynthia Rylant. Illustrated by Stephen Gammell.

King Bidgood's in the Bathtub by Audrey Wood. Illustrated by Don Wood.

1987 *Hey, Al* by Arthur Yorinks. Illustrated by Richard Egielski.

Honor Books:

The Village of Round and Square Houses by Ann Grifalconi.

Alphabatics by Suse MacDonald.

Rumpelstiltskin by Paul O. Zelinsky.

1988 *Owl Moon* by Jane Yolen. Illustrated by John Schoenherr.

Honor Book:

Mufaro's Beautiful Daughters by John Steptoe.

1989 *Song and Dance Man* by Karen Ackerman. Illustrated by Stephen Gammell.

Honor Books:

Free Fall by David Wiesner.

Goldilocks and the Three Bears by James Marshall.

Mirandy and Brother Wind by Patricia McKissack.

The Boy and the Three-Year Nap by Diane Snyder. Illustrated by Allen Say.

1990 *Lon Po Po: A Red-Riding Hood Story from China* by Ed Young.

Honor Books:

Hershel and the Hanukkah Goblins by Eric Kimmel. Illustrated by Trina Schart Hyman.

The Talking Eggs by Robert D. San Souci. Illustrated by Jerry Pinkney.

Bill Peet: An Autobiography by Bill Peet.

Color Zoo by Lois Ehlert.

1991   *Black and White* by David Macaulay.

Honor Books:

Puss 'n Boots by Charles Perrault. Illustrated by Fred Marcellino.

"More, More, More," Said the Baby: 3 Love Stories by Vera B. Williams.

1992   *Tuesday* by David Wiesner.

Honor Book:

Tar Beach by Faith Ringgold.

1993   *Mirette on the High Wire* by Emily Arnold McCully.

Honor Books:

Seven Blind Mice by Ed Young.

The Stinky Cheese Man & Other Fairly Stupid Tales by Jon Scieszka. Illustrated by Lane Smith.

Working Cotton by Sherley Anne Williams. Illustrated by Carole Bayard.

1994   *Grandfather's Journey* by Allen Say.

Honor Books:

Peppe the Lamplighter by Elisa Bartone. Illustrated by Ted Lewin.

In the Small, Small Pond by Denise Fleming.

Owen by Kevin Henkes.

Raven: A Trickster Tale from the Pacific Northwest by Gerald McDermott.

Yo! Yes? by Chris Raschka.

1995   *Smoky Night* by Eve Bunting. Illustrated by David Diaz.

Honor Books:

Swamp Angel by Anne Isaacs. Illustrated by Paul O. Zelinsky.

John Henry by Julius Lester. Illustrated by Jerry Pinkney.

Time Flies by Eric Rohmann.

1996   *Officer Buckle and Gloria* by Peggy Rathman.

Honor Books:

Alphabet City by Stephen Johnson.

Zin! Zin! Zin! a Violin by Lloyd Moss. Illustrated by Marjorie Priceman.

The Faithful Friend by Robert D. San Souci. Illustrated by Brian Pinkney.

Tops and Bottoms by Janet Stevens.

1997   *Golem* by David Wisniewski.

Honor Books:

Hush! A Thai Lullaby by Minfong Ho. Illustrated by Holly Meade.

The Graphic Alphabet edited by Neal Porter. Illustrated by David Pelletier.

The Paperboy by Dav Pilkey.

Starry Messenger by Peter Sís.

Coretta Scott King Awards

The Coretta Scott King Awards are intended to commemorate the work of Dr. Martin Luther King, Jr., and his wife, Coretta Scott King. These awards are sponsored by the Social Responsibilities Round Table of the American Library Association. The Coretta Scott King Awards are presented annually to an outstanding African American children's author and, since 1974, to an African American illustrator of a picture book. More information about this award can be found in Henrietta Smith's *The Coretta Scott King Awards Book: From Vision to Reality,* published by the American Library Association.

1970   *Martin Luther King, Jr.: Man of Peace* by Lillie Patterson.

1971   *Black Troubador: Langston Hughes* by Charlemae H. Rollins.

1972   *17 Black Artists* by Elton C. Fax.

1973   *I Never Had It Made* by Jackie Robinson as told to Alfred Duckett.

1974   **Author Award:** *Ray Charles* by Sharon Bell Mathis.

   Illustrator Award: The same title, illustrated by George Ford.

1975   **Author Award:** *The Legend of Africana* by Dorothy Robinson.

   Illustrator Award: The same title, illustrated by Herbert Temple.

1976   **Author Award:** *Duey's Tale* by Pearl Bailey.

   Illustrator Award: No award given.

1977   **Author Award:** *The Story of Stevie Wonder* by James Haskins.

   Illustrator Award: No award given.

1978   **Author Award:** *Africa Dream* by Eloise Greenfield.

   Illustrator Award: The same title, illustrated by Carole Bayard.

1979   **Author Award:** *Escape to Freedom* by Ossie Davis.

   Illustrator Award: *Something on My Mind* by Nikki Grimes. Illustrated by Tom Feelings.

1980   **Author Award:** *The Young Landlords* by Walter Dean Myers.

   Illustrator Award: *Cornrows* by Camille Yarbrough. Illustrated by Carole Bayard.

1981   **Author Award:** *This Life* by Sidney Poitier.

   Illustrator Award: *Beat the Story-Drum, Pum-Pum* by Ashley Bryan.

1982   **Author Award:** *Let the Circle Be Unbroken* by Mildred D. Taylor.

   Illustrator Award: *Mother Crocodile: An Uncle Amadou Tale from Senegal* by Rosa Guy. Illustrated by John Steptoe.

1983   **Author Award:** *Sweet Whispers, Brother Rush* by Virginia Hamilton.

Illustrator Award: *Black Child* by Peter Mugabane.

1984   **Author Award:** *Everett Anderson's Good-Bye* by Lucille Clifton.

Illustrator Award: *My Mama Needs Me* by Mildred Pitts Walter. Illustrated by Pat Cummings.

1985   **Author Award:** *Motown and Didi* by Walter Dean Myers.

Illustrator Award: No award given.

1986   **Author Award:** *The People Could Fly: American Black Folktales* by Virginia Hamilton.

Illustrator Award: *Patchwork Quilt* by Valerie Flournoy. Illustrated by Jerry Pinkney.

1987   **Author Award:** *Justin and the Best Biscuits in the World* by Mildred Pitts Walter.

Illustrator Award: *Half Moon and One Whole Star* by Crescent Dragonwagon. Illustrated by Jerry Pinkney.

1988   **Author Award:** *The Friendship* by Mildred D. Taylor.

Illustrator Award: *Mufaro's Beautiful Daughters: An African Tale* by John Steptoe.

1989   **Author Award:** *Fallen Angels* by Walter Dean Myers.

Illustrator Award: *Mirandy and Brother Wind* by Patricia McKissack. Illustrated by Jerry Pinkney.

1990   **Author Award:** *A Long Hard Journey* by Patricia C. and Fredrick L. McKissack.

Illustrator Award: *Nathaniel Talking* by Eloise Greenfield. Illustrated by Jan Spivey Gilchrist.

1991   **Author Award:** *Road to Memphis* by Mildred D. Taylor.

Illustrator Award: *Aïda* by Leontyne Price. Illustrated by Leo and Diane Dillon.

1992   **Author Award:** *Now Is Your Time! The African-American Struggle for Freedom* by Walter Dean Myers.

Illustrator Award: *Tar Beach* by Faith Ringgold.

1993   **Author Award:** *The Dark-Thirty: Southern Tales of the Supernatural* by Patricia McKissack.

Illustrator Award: *Origins of Life on Earth: An African Creation Myth* by David A. Anderson. Illustrated by Kathleen Atkins Smith.

1994   **Author Award:** *Toning the Sweep* by Angela Johnson.

Illustrator Award: *Soul Looks Back in Wonder* compiled and illustrated by Tom Feelings.

1995   **Author Award:** *Christmas in the Big House, Christmas in the Quarters* by Patricia C. and Fredrick L McKissack.

Illustrator Award: *The Creation* by James Weldon Johnson. Illustrated by James E. Ransome.

1996   **Author Award:** *Her Stories* by Virgina Hamilton.

Illustrator Award: *The Middle Passage: White Ships Black Cargo* by Tom Feelings.

1997   **Author Award:** *Slam!* by Walter Dean Myers.

Illustrator Award: *Minty: A Story of Young Harriet Tubman* by Alan Schroeder. Illustrated by Jerry Pinkney.

Phoenix Award

Established in 1985 by the Children's Literature Association, the Phoenix Award is presented annually to the author (or the estate of the author) of a children's book that was published in English twenty years earlier which did not win a major award at the time of its original publication. Occasionally, the selectors of this award also name one or more honor books. More information about this award can be found in Alethea Helbig and Agnes Perkins's two-volume work *The Phoenix Award of the Children's Literature Association*, published by Scarecrow Press. Both the winners and the honor books are listed here.

1985   *The Mark of the Horse Lord* by Rosemary Sutcliff.

1986   *Queenie Peavy* by Robert Burch.

1987   *Smith* by Leon Garfield.

1988   *The Rider and His Horse* by Erik Christian Haugaard.

1989   *The Night Watchmen* by Helen Cresswell.
Honor Books:
Brother, Can You Spare a Dime? by Milton Meltzer.
Pistol by Adrienne Richard

1990   *Enchantress from the Stars* by Sylvia Louise Engdahl.
Honor Books:
Ravensgill by William Mayne
Sing Down the Moon by Scott O'Dell.

1991   *A Long Way from Verona* by Jane Gardam.
Honor Books:
A Game of Dark by William Mayne.
The Tombs of Atuan by Ursula LeGuin

1992   *A Sound of Chariots* by Mollie Hunter.

1993   *Carrie's War* by Nina Bawden.
Honor Book:
A Proud Taste for Scarlet and Miniver by E. L. Konigsburg.

1994   *Of Nightingales That Weep* by Katherine Paterson.

Honor Books:
My Brother Sam Is Dead by James L. and Christopher Collier.
Listen for the Fig Tree by Sharon Bell Mathis.

1995 *Dragonwings* by Laurence Yep.
Honor Book:
Tuck Everlasting by Natalie Babbitt.

1996 *The Stone Book* by Alan Garner.
Honor Book:
Abel's Island by William Steig.

1997 *I Am the Cheese* by Robert Cormier.

Other children's literature awards given in the United States

BOSTON GLOBE/HORN BOOK AWARDS Jointly sponsored by the *Boston Globe* and the *Horn Book Magazine*, these awards are presented annually to the creators of three outstanding children's books. One of the awards recognizes an excellent work of fiction, another honors a picture book with outstanding illustrations, and the third goes to an exceptional work of nonfiction. The fiction and illustration awards have been presented since 1967, and the nonfiction award has been given since 1976.

EDGAR ALLEN POE AWARD Sponsored by the Mystery Writers of America, this award is presented to the author of a mystery novel intended for children. This award has been given annually since 1961.

INTERNATIONAL READING ASSOCIATION CHILDREN'S BOOK AWARD Sponsored by the Institute for Reading Research and administered by the International Reading Association, this award honors a children's book by a new author who "shows unusual promise in the children's book field." This award has been given annually since 1975.

LAURA INGALLS WILDER AWARD Sponsored by the Association for Library Service to Children of the American Library Association, this award is intended to recognize a children's author or illustrator from the United States whose body of work has made a lasting contribution to children's literature. When this award was first established in the mid-1950s, it was presented every five years. Since the 1980, however, the award has been given every three years.

MILDRED L. BATCHELDER AWARD Sponsored by the Association for Library Service to Children of the American Library Association, this award honors children's books that have been translated into English and that originally appeared in a country other than the United States. This award has been given annually since 1968.

NATIONAL COUNCIL OF TEACHERS OF ENGLISH AWARD FOR EXCELLENCE IN POETRY FOR CHILDREN This award is intended to honor living poets from the United Sates whose works have made a lasting contribution to children's literature. When this award was established in 1977, it was given annually, but since 1982 it has been given every three years.

ORBIS PICTUS AWARD   Sponsored by the National Council of Teachers of English's Committee on Using Nonfiction in the Elementary Language Arts Classroom, this award is presented to the author of a work of nonfiction for children. The award has been given annually since 1990.

SCOTT O'DELL AWARD FOR HISTORICAL FICTION   Established by Scott O'Dell, this award is given to the author of an outstanding work of historical fiction set in North America and originally published in the United States. This award has been given annually since 1984.

Children's literature awards given in other countries

CARNEGIE MEDAL (Great Britain)   Sponsored by the British Library Association, this award is given to the author of an outstanding children's book first published in the United Kingdom during the preceding year. The Carnegie Medal has been given annually since 1937.

KATE GREENAWAY MEDAL (Great Britain)   Sponsored by the British Library Association, this award is given to the illustrator of an outstanding picture book first published in the United Kingdom during the preceding year. The Greenaway Medal has been given annually since 1957.

CANADIAN LIBRARY ASSOCIATION BOOK OF THE YEAR FOR CHILDREN (Canada) This award is given to the author of an outstanding children's book first published in Canada during the preceding year. Occasionally, a second award is given to an outstanding children's book written in French. Eligibility for this award is limited to Canadian citizens. This award has been given annually since 1947.

AMELIA FRANCES HOWARD-GIBBON MEDAL (Canada)   Sponsored by the Canadian Library Association, this award is given to the illustrator of an outstanding picture book first published in the Canada during the preceding year. Eligibility for this award is limited to Canadian citizens. This award has been given annually since 1971.

HANS CHRISTIAN ANDERSEN PRIZE   Sponsored by the International Board on Books for Young People, this award is given to a living author and, since 1976, to a living illustrator whose works have made significant international contributions to children's literature. This award has been given biennially since 1956.

Mark's Edition of the Adventures of Little Red Riding Hood. Published by Fisk & Little, Albany, New York, 1820.

Books About Children's Literature

Chapter 8

The following bibliography is not intended to be a comprehensive listing of every secondary source that deals with children's literature. Instead, I have attempted to assemble a list of important books that serve as good starting-off points for people interested in learning more about children's literature. I have emphasized more recent books, but I have also included many classic works in the field. I have not included any books that focus entirely on one children's author. There are many such works now in print, but anyone who is seeking these types of books can easily find them in any sizable library. One simply needs to conduct a search using the author's name as the subject listing. In order to make this bibliography more useful to readers, I have divided it into numerous categories, each with its own subheading.

The first category deals with books that take general or historical approaches to children's literature. This is followed by works on particular types or genres of children's books, such as picture books or historical fiction. The next category includes two sections of books focused on age groups—young children and adolescents. The next category focuses on issues, including multiculturalism, gender roles, and censorship. The final category relates to practical concerns, such as using children's literature in the classroom or serving children in libraries.

General or historical works on children's literature

General works

Butts, Dennis, ed. *Stories and Society: Children's Literature in Its Social Context.* London: Macmillan, 1992. The essays in this collection explore on social forces have influenced various types of children's literature, including school stories, adventure stories, and works of fantasy.

Egoff, Sheila, G. T. Stubbs, and L.F. Ashley, eds. *Only Connect: Readings on Children's Literature.* 2d ed. Toronto: Oxford University Press, 1980. This collection of essays covers a wide range of subjects, ranging from literary analyses of individual children's books to short histories of different forms of children's literature.

Hunt, Peter. *An Introduction to Children's Literature.* New York: Oxford University Press, 1994. Hunt discusses the history and important characteristics of children's literature.

Lanes, Selma G. *Down the Rabbit Hole: Adventures and Misadventures in the Realm of Children's Literature.* New York: Atheneum, 1980. In this collection of essays, Lanes discusses the literary merits of numerous classic children's books.

Laurie, Alison. *Don't Tell the Grown-ups: Subversive Children's Literature.* Boston: Little, Brown, 1990. In this collection of related essays, Laurie examines the antiauthoritarian themes found in many children's books.

Lehr, Susan, ed. *Battling Dragons: Issues and Controversy in Children's Literature.* Portsmouth, NH: Heinemann, 1995. The essays in this volume explain how children's literature is affected by such issues as censorship, sexism, and racism.

Nodelman, Perry. *The Pleasures of Children's Literature.* 2d ed. White Plains, NY: Longman, 1996. Often used as a textbook in children's literature courses, this book explores many of the cultural and ideological assumptions that underlie children's literature.

Wintle, Justin, and Emma Fisher: *The Pied Pipers: Interviews with the Influential Creators of Children's Literature.* New York: Paddington Press, 1974. This books contains interviews with many important children's authors, including John Rowe Townsend, Roald Dahl, Rummer Godden, Scott O'Dell, Judy Blume, Alan Garner, Madeleine L'Engle, Rosemary Sutcliff, and Leon Garfield.

General histories of children's literature

Bingham, Jane, and Grayce Scholt. *Fifteen Centuries of Children's Literature.* Westport, CT: Greenwood Press, 1976. Focusing on the history of British and American books for children, Bingham and Scholt do an especially good job of examining the origins of children's literature.

Hunt, Peter, ed. *Children's Literature: An Illustrated History.* New York: Oxford University Press, 1995. This lavishly illustrated work covers the history of children's literature throughout the English-speaking world.

Hürlimann, Bettina. *Three Centuries of Children's Books in Europe.* Translated by Brian Alderson. Cleveland: World, 1968. This is one of the few works that covers the history of children's literature from all the European countries.

Meigs, Cornelia, et al. *A Critical History of Children's Literature,* rev. ed. New York: Macmillan, 1969. Although this book covers the early history of British and American children's literature, the sections that deal with children's books written during the first half of the twentieth century are especially strong.

Townsend, John Rowe. *Written for Children: An Outline of English-Language Children's Literature.* 4th ed. New York: Harper, 1992. Townsend provides a concise history of children's literature and includes a discussion of contemporary books.

History of British children's literature

Carpenter, Humphrey. *Secret Gardens: A Study of the Golden Age of Children's Literature.* Boston: Houghton Mifflin, 1985. This work examines the classic children's books written in England during the late Victorian and Edwardian periods.

Darton, F. J. Harvery. *Children's Books in England: Five Centuries of Social Life.* 2d ed. Cambridge: Cambridge University Press, 1982. One of the classic works in the field, this book does an excellent job of placing the history of British children's literature in its social and cultural contexts.

Green, Roger Lancelyn. *Teller of Tales.* 2d ed. New York: Ward, 1965. Green discusses the lives and contributions of many important English authors of children's books.

Jackson, Mary V. *Engines of Instruction, Mischief, and Magic: Children's Literature in England from Its Beginnings to 1839.* Omaha: University of Nebraska Press, 1990. Although this volume does not match the scholarly breadth of Darton's book, it provides information on some early children's books that Darton does not discuss.

McGavran, James Holt, Jr. ed. *Romanticism and Children's Literature in Nineteenth-Century England.* Athens, GA: University of Georgia Press, 1991. The essays in this volume cover the image of the romantic child in the writings of William Wordsworth, Samuel Taylor Coleridge, Maria Edgeworth, and several other Romantic and Victorian authors.

Muir, Percy. *English Children's Books, 1600-1900.* New York: Praeger, 1954. Muir's discussions of individual titles are especially insightful.

Pickering, Samuel. *John Locke and Children's Books in Eighteenth-Century England.* Knoxville, TN: University Press of Tennessee, 1981. Pickering explains how the ideas of the philosopher John Locke helped shape British children's literature.

Thwaite, Mary. *From Primer to Pleasure in Reading: An Introduction to the History of Children's Books in England.* 2nd ed. Boston: Horn Book, 1972. This work covers the history of British children's literature from the advent of printing to the beginning of World War I.

History of American children's literature

Avery, Gillian. *Behold the Child: American Children and Their Books, 1621-1922.* Baltimore: Johns Hopkins, 1995. Avery tells the history of American children's literature from the perspective of a British writer and critic, often comparing American children's books to their British counterparts.

Cart, Michael. *What's So Funny: Wit and Humor in American Children's Literature.* New York: HarperCollins, 1995. Cart examines the use of humor in historical as well as contemporary American children's literature.

Griswold, Jerry. ***Audacious Kids: Coming of Age in America's Classic Children's Books.*** New York: Oxford University Press, 1992. Griswold discusses twelve classic children's books written during the nineteenth and early twentieth centuries.

Jordan, Alice M. ***From Rollo to Tom Sawyer.*** Boston: Horn Book, 1948. In this classic work, Jordan traces the development of American children's literature from the 1830s to the 1870s.

MacLeod, Anne Scott. ***American Childhood: Essays in Children's Literature of the Nineteenth and Twentieth Centuries.*** Athens, GA: University of Georgia Press, 1994. The essays in this collection deal with a wide variety of subjects related to the history of American children's literature, including censorship and the changing portrayal of parents in children's literature.

———. ***A Moral Tale: Children's Fiction and American Culture, 1820-1860.*** Hamden, CT: Archon, 1975. MacLeod explains how changes in American society affected the children's literature of the period.

West, Mark I. ***Children, Culture, and Controversy.*** Hamden, CT: Archon, 1988. This work examines some of the major controversies in the history of American children's literature.

Literary criticism and children's literature

Hunt, Peter, ed. ***Literature for Children: Contemporary Criticism.*** New York: Routledge, 1992. Written by some of the leading critics in the field, the essays in this collection provide good examples of how various forms of literary criticism can be used to analyze children's literature.

McGillis, Roderick. ***The Nimble Reader: Literary Theory and Children's Literature.*** New York: Twayne Publishers, 1996. McGillis shows how the major schools of criticism have approached children's literature, including Formalism, New Criticism, and Poststructuralism.

May, Jill P. ***Children's Literature and Critical Theory.*** New York: Oxford University Press, 1995. May begins her book by explaining how many different forms of literary criticism have been used to interpret children's literature, but she focuses most of the book on applying reader response theory to various children's books.

Children literature genres

Picture books

Bader, Barbara. ***American Picturebooks from Noah's Ark to The Beast Within.*** New York: Macmillan, 1976. Bader provides a concise history of American picture books and analyzes a number of important picture books.

Manna, Anthony, and Carolyn Brodie, eds. ***Art & Story: The Role of Illustration in Multicultural Literature for Youth.*** Fort Atkinson, WI: Highsmith Press, 1997. The contributors to this volume, many of whom are professional illustrators, explore the importance of visual images in multicultural literature for children.

Nodelman, Perry. ***Words about Pictures: The Narrative Art of Picture Books.*** Athens, GA: University of Georgia Press, 1988. Nodleman carefully examines the interrelationship between visual images and text in many important picture books.

Sendak, Maurice. ***Caldecott and Co.: Notes on Books and Pictures.*** New York: Farrar, Straus, and Giroux, 1988. Sendak discusses his own picture books as well as the works of other major contributors to the art of picture books, including Randolph Caldecott and Beatrix Potter.

Stewig, John Warren. ***Looking at Picture Books.*** Fort Atkinson, WI: Highsmith Press, 1995. In this richly illustrated volume, Stewig provides an aesthetic analysis of picture books, examining such issues as book design, the use of color, and the compositional components of illustrations.

Historical and contemporary realism

Cordier, M. H. and M. Perez-Stable. ***Peoples of the American West: Historical Perspectives Through Children's Literature.*** Metuchen, NJ: Scarecrow Press, 1989. This book provides a survey of historical fiction set in the American West and suggests ways these books can be used to teach children about American history.

deJovine, F. Anthony. ***The Young Hero in American Fiction.*** New York: Appleton-Century, 1971. This book includes discussions of the heroes from several realistic books for young readers.

Fisher, Margery ***The Bright Face of Danger: An Exploration of the Adventure Story.*** Boston: Horn Book, 1986. Fisher discusses the nature and appeal of realistic adventure stories for children.

Wilkin, Binnie Tate. ***Survival Themes in Fiction for Children and Young People.*** Metuchen, NJ: Scarecrow Press, 1978. Wilkin discusses numerous realistic children's books in which the central characters face danger.

Fantasy literature

Anderson, Celia Catlett, and Marilyn Fair Apseloff. ***Nonsense Literature for Children: Aesop to Seuss.*** Hamden, CT: Library Professional Publications, 1989. The authors discuss the nature and appeal of nonsense literature and analyze the works of several major figures in this subgenre of fantasy literature.

Antczak, Janice. ***Science Fiction: The Mythos of a New Romance.*** New York: Neal-Schuman, 1985. Antczk examines the nature and history of science fiction for children and young adults.

Attebery, Brian. ***The Fantasy Tradition in American Children's Literature.*** Bloomington, IN: Indiana University Press, 1980. Attebery traces the history of American fantasy literature for children, and discusses the contributions of several important writers, such L. Frank Baum and Ursual K. Le Guin.

Egoff, Sheila. ***Worlds Within: Children's Fantasy from the Middle Ages to Today.***

Chicago: American Library Association. Egoff surveys the history of this genre of children's literature.

Goldthwaite, John. *The Natural History of Make-Believe.* New York: Oxford University Press, 1996. Goldthwaite traces the evolution of fantasy literature from its roots in folklore to its most modern manifestations.

Gose, Elliott. *Mere Creatures: A Study of Modern Fantasy Literature for Children.* Toronto: University of Toronto Press, 1988. This work explores some of the mythic elements in contemporary fantasy literature.

Kuznets, Lois. *When Toys Come Alive: Narratives of Animations, Metamorphosis and Development.* New Haven, CT: Yale University Press, 1994. Kuznets analyzes numerous children's books that feature anthropomorphic toys and puppets, including *Pinocchio, Winnie the Pooh,* and *The Mouse and His Child.*

Sales, Roger. *Fairy Tales and After: From Snow White to E. B. White.* Cambridge, MA: Harvard University Press, 1978. Sales explores how fairy tales have influenced fantasy literature for children.

Sullivan, C. W. III. *Welsh Celtic Myth in Modern Fantasy.* Westport, CT: Greenwood Press, 1989. Sullivan explains how J. R. R. Tolkien, Lloyd Alexander, and other children's fantasy writers drew on Celtic sources.

Fairy tales and folklore

Bettelheim, Bruno. *The Uses of Enchantment: The Meaning and Importance of Fairy Tales.* New York: Knopf, 1976. Drawing on psychoanalytic theory, Bettelheim explores the psychological dimensions of fairy tales.

Blatt, Gloria, ed. *Once Upon a Folktale: Capturing the Folklore Process with Children.* New York: Teachers College Press, 1993. The essays in this collection suggest various ways to introduce children to folklore.

von Franz, Marie Louise. *The Feminine in Fairy Tales.* New York: Spring, 1972. In this book, von Franz applies some of the theories of Carl Jung to fairy tales.

Yolen, Jane. *Touch Magic: Fantasy, Faerie and Folklore in the Literature of Childhood.* New York: Philomel, 1981. The essays in this book deal with the history of folklore and its bearing on children's lives.

Zipes, Jack. *Breaking the Magic Spell: Radical Theories of Folk and Fairy Tales.* Austin, TX: University of Texas Press, 1979. This is the first of several books in which Zipes examines the sociohistorical forces that came into play when oral folktales were transformed into published fairy tales.

Poetry and nursery rhymes

Copeland, Jerry S. *Speaking of Poets: Interviews with Poets Who Write for Children and Young Adults.* Urbana, IL: National Council of Teachers of English, 1993. The sixteen poets who are represented in this book all discuss their approaches to writing poetry for young readers.

Hopkins, Lee Bennett. ***Pass the Poetry, Please!*** 2d ed. New York: Harper, 1987. Hopkins discusses how poetry can be introduced to children.

Livingston, Myra. ***Climb into the Bell Tower: Essays on Poetry.*** New York: Harper-Collins, 1990. This is one of several books in which Livingston explores the nature and value of poetry for children.

Rollin, Lucy. ***Cradle and All: A Cultural and Psychoanalytic Study of Nursery Rhymes.*** Jackson, MS: University Press of Mississippi, 1992. Rollin discusses the appeal and cultural significance of many popular nursery rhymes.

Series books and popular culture for children

Billman, Carol. ***Secret of the Stratemeyer Syndicate: Nancy Drew, the Hardy Boys and the Million Dollar Fiction Factory.*** New York: Ungar, 1986. Billman explores the history of series books and discusses the appeal of this type of children's literature.

Daniels, Les. *Comix: **A History of Comic Books in America.*** New York: Bonanza Books, 1971. Daniels traces the evolution of comic books and discusses their appeal as well as the controversy surrounding them.

Johnson, Deidre. ***Edward Stratemeyer and the Stratemeyer Syndicate.*** New York: Twayne, 1993. In addition to explaining how Edward Stratemeyer created and oversaw the production of thousands of series books, Johnson comments on several of the largely unknown authors who helped write these books.

Jones, Daryl. ***The Dime Novel Western.*** Bowling Green, Ohio: Popular Press, 1978. Jones examines the history, nature, and popularity of dime novels.

Film adaptations of children's books

Rollin, Lucy, ed. ***The Antic Art: Enhancing Children's Literary Experiences Through Film and Video.*** Fort Atkinson, WI: Highsmith Press, 1993. This collection includes essays about film adaptations of children's books as well as essays on how to incorporate films and video into classroom activities.

Sharkey, Paulette Boching. ***Newbery and Caldecott Medal and Honor Books in Other Media.*** New York: Neal-Schuman, 1992. Sharkey provides lots of factual information about film and video versions of many award-winning children's books.

Street, Douglas, ed. ***Children's Novels and the Movies.*** New York: Ungar, 1983. The contributors to this volume compare the film and book versions of twenty-four classics for children.

Age groupings

Literature for young children

Burke, Eileen. ***Literature for the Young Child.*** Boston: Allyn & Bacon, 1990. Burke discusses the value of sharing literature with preschoolers and provides suggestions for how parents and teachers can enhance preschoolers' experiences with books.

Butler, Dorothy. *Babies Need Books.* 2d ed. New York: Penguin, 1988. Taking a personal and passionate approach, Butler argues that young children greatly benefit from interacting with books.

Glazer, Joan I. *Literature for Young Children.* 3rd ed. Upper Saddle River, NJ: Merrill/Prentice Hall, 1991. Glazer provides lots of information on how literature helps young children acquire language skills and supports their emotional and intellectual development.

White, Dorothy. *Books Before Five.* Oxford: Oxford University Press, 1954. In this classic study, White thoughtfully analyzes her preschool-aged daughter's reactions to over one hundred books.

Literature for adolescents

Cart, Michael. *From Romance to Realism: Fifty Years of Growth and Change in Young Adult Literature.* New York: HarperCollins, 1996. This ground-breaking book provides the first thorough history of literature for adolescents.

Donnelson, Kenneth L, and Alleen Pace Nilsen. *Literature for Today's Young Adults.* 4th ed. Glenview, IL: Scott, Foresman, 1989. Often used as a textbook in courses on young adult literature, this book provides an excellent survey of important works written for adolescent readers.

Estes, Sally, ed. *Growing Up Is Hard to Do.* Chicago: American Library Association, 1994. This short book includes several useful bibliographies of young adult novels dealing with particular themes, such as "Growing Up Female," "Growing Up Religious," and "Growing Up Gay-Aware."

Vandergrift, Kay E, ed. *Mosaics of Meaning: Enhancing the Intellectual Life of Young Adults Through Story.* Lanham, MD: Scarecrow Press, 1996. The contributors to this volume explore how young adults use literature to give their lives meaning.

Special issues and topics

Multiculturalism and children's literature

Johnson, Lauri, and Sally Smith. *Dealing with Diversity through Multicultural Fiction: Library-Classroom Partnerships.* Chicago: American Library Association, 1993. The authors show how multicultural literature can be used to expose and counter children's negative attitudes to cultural differences.

Lindgren, Merri V., ed. *The Multicolored Mirror: Cultural Substance in Literature for Children and Young Adults.* Fort Atkinson, WI: Highsmith Press, 1991. In this volume, a variety of educators, children's authors, illustrators, and publishers discuss the importance of multicultural literature for young readers.

Manna, Anthony and Carolyn Brodie, eds. *Many Faces, Many Voices: Multicultural Literary Experiences for Youth.* Fort Atkinson, WI, 1992. This work provides a solid introduction to multicultural literature for children.

Rochman, Hazel. *Against Borders: Promoting Books for a Multicultural World.* Chicago: American Library Association, 1993. Rochman discusses numerous books representing a variety of ethnic groups and explains how these books can be used to help young people understand and appreciate the cultures of ethnic groups other than their own.

African Americans and children's literature

Johnson, Dianne. *Telling Tales: The Pedagogy and the Promise of African-American Literature for Youth.* Westport, CT: Greenwood Press, 1990. In addition to analyzing the works of several prominent African American children's authors, Johnson discusses W. E. B. DuBois's efforts to promote literature for African American children.

Simms, Rudine. Shadow and Substance: *Afro-American Experience in Contemporary Children's Fiction.* Urbana, IL: National Council of Teachers of English, 1982. Sims examines the images of African American in 150 realistic children's books published between 1965 and 1979.

Smith, Karen Patricia, ed. *African American Voices in Young Adult Literature: Tradition, Transition, Transformation.* Metuchen, NJ: Scarecrow, 1994. The contributors to this volume examine the contributions of African American writers to young adult literature.

American Indians and children's literature

Hirschfelder, Arlene B., ed. *American Indian Stereotypes in the World of Children: A Reader and Bibliography.* Metuchen, NJ: Scarecrow, 1982. The contributors to this volume examine the negative images of American Indians found in many children's books.

Slapin, Beverly, and Doris Seale, eds. *Through Indian Eyes: The Native Experience in Books for Children.* Philadelphia: New Society Publishers, 1992. The contributors to this volume discuss children's literature written by American Indians.

Stott, Jon C. *Native Americans in Children's Literature.* Phoenix, AZ: Oryx, 1995. Stott discusses the roles that American Indians play in children's books from the United States and Canada.

Gender roles in children's literature

Foster, Shirley, and Judy Simons. *What Katy Read: Feminist Rereadings of "Classic" Stories for Girls.* Iowa City: University of Iowa Press. Foster and Simons argue that children's books by Louisa May Alcott and other writers for girls often support feminist positions.

Nelson, Claudia. *Boys Will Be Girls: The Feminine Ethic and British Children's Fiction, 1857-1917.* New Brunswick, New Jersey: Rutgers University Press, 1991. Nelson carefully examines gender roles in Victorian children's literature.

White, Barbara A. *Growing Up Female: Adolescent Girlhood in American Fiction.*

Westport, CT: Greenwood Press, 1985. White examines numerous books that feature adolescent female characters and analyzes these characters' experiences in an effort to define female socialization patterns.

Censorship and children's literature

Moffett, James. *Storm in the Mountains: A Case Study of Censorship, Conflict and Consciousness.* Carbondale, IL: Southern Illinois University Press, 1988, Moffett examines the inner workings of a censorship case that took place in Kanawha County, West Virginia.

Simmons, John S., ed. *Censorship: A Threat to Reading, Learning, Thinking.* Newark, DE: International Reading Association, 1994. This book covers numerous censorship cases and provides information on how to deal with attempts to ban children's books.

West, Mark I. *Trust Your Children: Voices Against Censorship Children's Literature.* 2d ed. New York: Neal-Schuman, 1997. Features interviews with numerous censored children's authors, including Katherine Paterson, Phyllis Reynolds Naylor, Gail Haley, Judy Blume, Maurice Sendak, John Steptoe and Roald Dahl.

Library and classroom

Using children's literature in the classroom

Coody, Betty. *Using Literature with Young Children.* 5th ed. Dubuque, IA: Brown and Benchmark, 1997. This book is full of practical advice on how to incorporate children's literature into the educational programs for preschoolers and children in the early grades of elementary school.

Cullinan, B. E., ed. *Children's Literature in the Reading Program.* Newark, DE: International Reading Association, 1987. The contributors to this volume discuss the value of literature-based reading programs and provide information on how to implement such programs.

Harris, V. J., ed. *Teaching Multicultural Literature in Grades K–8.* Norwood, MA: Christopher-Gordon Publishers, 1993. The contributors in this book provide insights into how teachers can incorporate multicultural children's literature in their curricular plans.

Sloan, Glenna Davis. *The Child as Critic.* 3rd ed. New York: Teachers College Press, 1991. Sloan explains how literary theory can be used to enhance literature-based teaching.

Wood, Karen, and Anita Moss, eds. *Exploring Literature in the Classroom: Contents and Methods.* Norwood, MA: Christopher-Gordon Publishers, 1992. The contributors to this volume discuss the various ways that literature can be incorporated into the elementary school curriculum.

Library services for children

Barnett, Diana. *Everything You Need to Know About the School Library Media Center.* Fort Atkinson, WI: Highsmith Press, 1995. This practical handbook covers such subjects as helping students and their teachers, and selecting children's books.

Broderick, Dorothy M. *Library Work with Children.* New York: H. W. Wilson Co., 1977. With this book, Broderick influenced much of the recent thinking about library services for children.

Fasick, Adele M. *Managing Children's Services in the Public Library.* Englewood, CO: Libraries Unlimited, 1991. Fasick provides insights into the administrative aspects of running library programs for children.

Greene, Ellin. *Books, Babies, and Libraries: Serving Infants, Toddlers, Their Parents and Caregivers.* Chicago: American Library Association, 1991. Greene provides practical information on how librarians can play a positive role children's early learning as well as in parent education.

Jeffery, Debby Ann. *Literate Beginnings: Programs for Babies and Toddlers.* Chicago: American Library Association, 1995. This book features many programming ideas and activities that librarians can do with very young children.

Jones, Patrick. *Connecting Young Adults and Libraries: A How-to-Do-It Manual.* New York: Neal-Schuman Publishers, 1992. Jones provides practical information on how librarians can better serve young adults.

Van Orden, Phyllis. *Library Service to Children: A Guide to the Research, Planning, and Policy Literature.* Chicago: American Library Association, 1992. This work serves as an excellent guide to the various resources needed by children's librarians.

Teaching children's literature courses to adults

Sadler, Glenn Edward, ed. *Teaching Children's Literature: Issues, Pedagogy, Resources.* New York: Modern Language Association, 1992. The contributors to this volume discuss issues that often come up in children's literature courses and provide suggestions for different ways to teach such courses.

Lundin, Anne H., and Carol W. Cubberley. *Teaching Children's Literature: A Resource Guide, with a Directory of Courses.* Jefferson, NC: McFarland, 1995. Lundin and Cubberley provide lots of practical information, such as a survey of children's literature textbooks and a sampling of eight syllabi from children's literature courses.

Writing for children

Paterson, Katherine. *A Sense of Wonder: On Reading and Writing Books for Children.* New York: Plume/Penguin, 1995. In this collection of essays, Paterson shares her ideas about writing for children and discusses the origins of many of her award-winning children's books.

Zinsser, William, ed. ***Worlds of Childhood: The Art and Craft of Writing for Children.*** Boston: Houghton Mifflin, 1990. This book contains essays on writing for children by several prominent children's authors, including Jean Fritz, Jack Prelutsky, Maurice Sendak, and Rosemary Wells.

Index

Title Index

Author / Illustrator Index

Organization Index